Open Immediately!

Straight Talk on Direct Mail Fundraising:
What Works, What Doesn't, and Why

Open
Immediately!

Straight Talk on

Direct Mail Fundraising

What Works,
What Doesn't,
and Why

Stephen Hitchcock

Emerson
& Church
PUBLISHERS

First printed February 2004

10 9 8 7 6 5 4 3 2 1

Printed in the United States of America

This text is printed on acid-free paper.

Emerson & Church, Publishers
P.O. Box 338 • Medfield, MA 02052
Tel. 508-359-0019 • Fax 508-359-2703
www.contributionsmagazine.com

Library of Congress Cataloging-in-Publication Data

Hitchcock, Stephen
   Open Immediately! : straight talk on direct mail fundraising : what works, what doesn't, and why / Stephen Hitchcock
      p.cm
   ISBN 1-889102-12-1 (alk. paper)
      1. Fund raising. 2. Advertising, Direct-mail. 3. Nonprofit organizations--Finance. 4. Charities--Finance. I. Title

HV41.2.H58 2004
658.15'224--dc22   2003064312

THE AUTHOR

Stephen Hitchcock is President of Mal Warwick and Associates, Inc., where he has worked since 1986. The firm, which has its office in Berkeley, California, provides consulting services in direct response fundraising for regional and national nonprofit organizations.

Mr. Hitchcock, co-author with Mal Warwick of *Ten Steps to Fundraising Success*, has conducted workshops for both regional and national conferences of the Association of Fundraising Professionals. He has also taught seminars and workshops sponsored by the Public Broadcasting Service, National Public Radio, the Trust for Public Land, American Cancer Society, and Planned Parenthood. Each January he leads a Major Donor Fundraising Clinic.

His column about direct mail fundraising appears regularly in *Contributions* magazine, and his articles have been published in *Grass Roots Fundraising Journal* and *Successful Direct Mail and Telephone Fundraising*.

FOREWORD

Once upon a time, the people who wrote books were those who had the *time* to write books. They were monks, or nobles, or ... you get the point. They had something going for them.

Well, I've been lucky that way. Stephen Hitchcock's hard work and his involvement in the leadership of Mal Warwick & Associates have given me the time and opportunity to devote to thinking and writing. Because Steve has set me free from so much of the usual hullabaloo of running a consulting firm, I've been able to write 15 books and edit a bimonthly newsletter for more than 13 years now. More than that, Steve has encouraged me to do this work, and he's always full of good ideas about how to get my books more widely distributed.

That enthusiasm is based on Steve's passion for learning, his belief that this profession of raising money should be based on rigorous research and guided by robust conceptualization. Yes, direct mail fundraising is a practical, hands-on business, but it works much more effectively when it's based on information and insights. Steve's view is that both the organizations we work for and the donors who support those organizations are better served if *everyone* involved acquires as much knowledge as possible. So I hope you'll do yourself the favor of reading this important new book.

The real value of this book is that it distills nearly three decades of first-hand experience in direct mail fundraising. You'll find no wishful thinking or untried theories here. In our consulting firm, Steve is the one who is constantly poring over the actual results of all the mailings we send out, and we can always count on him for that obnoxious question, "Well, what does our testing say about this?"

In the pages that follow, you'll also discover the valuable lesson that successful nonprofit organizations have learned: creativity in the writing and design of direct mail is important, but to succeed in the long term, you must diligently manage and continuously evaluate your direct mail *program*. What counts is the thoughtful *scheduling* of a series of mailings that gives your donors enough different opportunities to support your organization.

Behind the good-natured admonitions and hard-headed advice you'll find in the book is the insight that direct mail fundraising is actually a self-reinforcing system or an ongoing process in which a diverse set of factors interact in an almost organic way. Direct response fundraising is the means by which donors and organizations *interact with each other*. In this process, donors and nonprofit staff become involved – in many positive ways – in each other's ongoing lives over a long period of time.

Steve and I have discovered that this multi-faceted interactive involvement is most productive when it is aimed at a strategic end. When your donors or prospective donors come to understand and participate in your organization's mission, then fundraising plays a key role in fulfilling that mission. And when the techniques you use to foster donors' participation are congruent with your organization's primary goals and key objectives, then your fundraising produces the greatest results for the organization.

That insight reflects the final quality that makes this book so useful. It's written by someone who really cares about nonprofit organizations and believes in philanthropy. Every year, Steve tops the list of those who use our company's matching gift program, and we're all amazed by the sample mailings of those organizations that Steve and his wife Jan so generously support.

All those contributions are probably your best guarantee that the time you take to read this book won't be wasted.

Berkeley, California Mal Warwick

INTRODUCTION

My first job in fundraising was a work study assignment in the development department for the graduate school I was attending. When I showed up that first day, the development director handed me a file and told me my job was to draft personalized thank you letters in response to individual gifts.

What a great way to get started in this weird and wonderful business of raising money by mail. I hope this book serves, in part, as a "thank you" to that first development director – as well as to all those extraordinary individuals who have sent checks in response to letters I've written over the years.

A profound sense of gratitude is the foundation for effective direct mail fundraising. That's because direct mail targets invitations and appeals to those individuals who are so generous and trusting that they will send checks through the mail – in most cases to individuals and organizations they've never seen.

That's why you'll find so much of this book devoted to thanking and cultivating the individuals and families in your organization's database – including making sure your letters include sincere expressions of gratitude for the donor's interest and generosity.

Whether you're a newcomer or a seasoned pro, I hope you'll you be both challenged and encouraged by what I've come to see as essential building blocks of direct mail fundraising:

1) No matter how brilliant your prose or how creative the design, the most important element about a mailing is that it goes out on a timely basis. Direct mail works because it is a *schedule of mailings* that, in the course of a calendar year, provides donors with enough opportunities to support organizations and issues they care about.

2) In your mailings, the *letter* – one that we hope is friendly, informative, persuasive, and readable – is the most important element. Brochures and other inserts can often suppress response, and a mailing without a letter hardly ever works.

3) In general, fancy formats – large envelopes, glossy paper, lots of inserts, premiums – are effective only for very large organizations. If you have 10,000 or fewer donors (perhaps even 50,000 or fewer), you can't afford those costly mailing packages. And it's likely that the donors attracted to your organization won't be persuaded by these visual bribes and promised premiums.

4) The fastest and surest way to boost income from your direct mail program is to *spend more money on your most generous and recent donors* – and less on those who give smaller dollar amounts. If individuals are sending you checks of $100, they are much more likely to keep doing that – and even increase their gifts – if you send personalized letters in closed-face envelopes with a live postage stamp on the return envelope and first class postage on the outer envelope.

5) Very, very few organizations can depend solely on income from direct mail to sustain their operations and programs. Mailings cost too much, and the checks donors send don't offset that investment. The rationale for direct mail is that it's the most cost effective way to a build a broad base of individuals.

Some of these direct-mail acquired donors can be cultivated for five-, six-, and seven-figure gifts. For others, it's more appropriate to invite them to become monthly donors through pre-authorized electronic funds transfer or credit card debt.

And the real pay-off in direct mail fundraising comes when long-time members or donors are encouraged to remember your organization with charitable bequests.

6) An annual membership or donor *renewal* series – with two, three, or more reminders – is the most efficient way to keep your donors or members active. These mailings should be simple and straightforward, with a very clear message that in one way or another says, "Now is the time to renew your membership (or your annual support)." At the end of the series of reminders, the message is even more blunt: "We haven't heard from you this year" or "We haven't yet received your annual gift."

7) Direct mail fundraising works only if you are continuously *acquiring new members or donors*. Those who respond to your letters are generous but they are, in most cases, older. They retire, they move away, and they pass away. Sending out mailings to "prospects" (those who give to other organizations but not yours or who subscribe to magazines) is expensive and complicated. But you must do it – preferably several times a year.

I learned these lessons because I've had wonderful teachers in the three decades I've been involved in nonprofit fundraising. I'm especially grateful to Mal Warwick and my other colleagues at the consulting firm where I've worked now for 17 years. I'm challenged by their fierce intelligence and inspired by their enthusiastic dedication to our clients. And I've had the great fortune to work with dozens of organizations – some for two decades – and I've seen how much they have benefited from the systematic use of direct mail.

My best and inspiring laboratory, though, has been my family: my own parents Cliff and De Hitchcock and my wife Jan, daughter Rachel, and son Nathan. Watching and listening to them as they respond to mailings and as they talk about the organizations they support – that has been the source of so many insights that have found their way into this book.

And, of course, there couldn't have been a book without Jerry Cianciolo and Kathy Brennan of *Contributions*, which provided the original forum for the material appearing in this book. Month after month, they've sent me the most interesting questions to answer. Their gentle (and repeated!) reminders about deadlines and their enthusiastic praise have created a fertile garden plot where I can grow larger ideas and specific suggestions.

If you choose to read these 81 chapters in sequential order, you'll find similar material and repetitious advice. Like a good fundraising letter, key concepts and specific advice appear in more than one place. I've decided to leave in these repetitions so that readers can open the book to any page and find a chapter that stands by itself – for quick reference or focused reading.

Thank you for reading the pages that follow!

Berkeley, California   Stephen Hitchcock

CONTENTS

PART II · ACQUIRING AND RENEWING DONORS

PART III · TARGETING YOUR MAILINGS

PART IV · WRITING EFFECTIVE LETTERS

PART V · KEY COMPONENTS OF YOUR APPEAL

PART VI · HOW TO ASK

I.

ESSENTIALS OF DIRECT MAIL FUNDRAISING

Your organization can raise more money now – and in the future – because one of the most effective forms of fundraising is also the most predictable.

I've had the good fortune to work for nearly two decades with a consulting firm that has compiled reams of statistical results. In the last few years, we've also carried out several research projects about the true value of donors acquired and renewed through direct mail. The patterns are startlingly similar, the trends amazingly constant, and the variances seemingly insignificant.

But this predictability and stability are a result not a cause. Direct mail fundraising works effectively, but only if you stick to the basics. You must observe some fundamental guidelines, and avoid some common pitfalls.

In the pages that follow, you'll discover the key principles that make direct mail an effective fundraising tool. In other words, to succeed at this work, you need to understand *why* donors respond

spond to direct mail – and why mailings are constructed and scheduled the way they are.

As you read this section, though, I hope you won't be looking for any hard-and-fast rules or eternal truths. They don't exist. In fact, one of our guiding principles is that what works for one organization may not work for another. That's why we *test* and then pay attention to actual results – not just to our intuitions or impressions. And why we experiment with new content and new formats – careful, calculated experiments not foolish wholesale change.

I also hope you'll come to the conclusion that the key ingredients in successful fundraising are patience and persistence. Direct mail works because it is an activity that is repeated again and again over long periods of time. It is a present investment that pays dividends in the future – months from now and even years from now.

Please, then, look upon these basic principles as allies in your organization's essential – and enjoyable – effort to build long-term relationships with donors who will give you more now and in the years to come.

1.

Top 10 Truths about Direct Mail Fundraising

Over the years, I've had the opportunity to study results of thousands of individual fund raising appeals and to review fund raising programs for hundreds of organizations. In the process, I've learned that there are some things that are almost always true.

These are "rules" that you should break after only careful consideration of your circumstances and your organization's tolerance for risk.

Here are my top 10 truths about direct mail fundraising:

1) Sending out thank you letters as quickly as possible is the single most important factor in insuring the success of your direct mail fundraising program.

2) Those organizations that raise the most money year after year have direct mail fundraising *programs* - not just a collection of appeal letters. What makes the difference is not the response rate or total income of any one mailing but rather the total number of gifts and the overall income generated by an annual schedule of mailings - with adequate time between mailings and with a

variation in the format or content of those mailings.

3) Asking your donors or members too often increases the rate at which those donors or members lapse, but organizations that don't send enough appeals see even more donors lapse.

4) Fundraising appeals work best when there is a letter, a separate reply device, and a reply or return envelope. All three are essential.

5) Enclosures - especially brochures - always slow down the process of getting out your mailing, increase your cost, and rarely generate enough income or increase response rates enough to justify the time and money you spend on them. In many instances, enclosures *reduce* response rates. Of course, there are exceptions to this rule, and often enclosures make executive directors and board members happy - and they're the ones who approve your fundraising budget.

6) Organizations that send out newsletters and informational mailings - not just solicitation letters - generate more income from their direct mail program.

7) Appeals related to true emergencies or a pressing crisis always bring in more gifts and more money than appeals for institutional purposes or for support of ongoing programs. However, direct mail programs that include institutional appeals - membership renewal, annual giving clubs, and annual report mailings - have higher donor retention and higher overall income.

8) Very, very few donors upgrade their giving. The first gift you receive from an individual is likely to be the amount written on subsequent checks. And a significant minority of donors decrease the amount of their gifts (in other words, an individual makes an initial gift of $100 but her next gift is only $50). Fortunately, gifts

from the precious few donors who do go on to increase their giving more than offset those who decrease their giving.

9) Your organization's donor-base must include both "large" and "small" donors - those who regularly contribute $1000 as well as those who send in $10 bills. Fundraising is democracy in action - you have to let everyone participate at the level he or she wishes.

10) Testing random samples of members with variations in letters or packages (for example, testing yellow reply envelope against a standard white reply envelope) almost never produces statistically valid differences in response rate. Yet, if you are regularly mailing more than 10,000 pieces of mail at any one time, testing will always provide valuable information that will reduce your mailing costs and, in some cases, boost your overall income.

2.

Hairsplitting Traps to Avoid

The key to success in direct mail fundraising is making sure you have a schedule that includes enough mailings to give your donors, and prospective donors, sufficient opportunities to support your organization. If you're spending all your time trying to make each mailing perfect, you won't be able to get out all your mailings.

The other danger of hairsplitting is that you could end up spending too much money on paper stock, laser personalization, or graphic design. It's unlikely that your more expensive mailing will produce enough income to offset the extra cost or generate enough additional returns to keep your membership or donor database growing.

Spending extra money, testing lots of variables — and hairsplitting in general — *does* make sense for those organizations that mail in *large* volumes and have very large donor bases. And, if your organization is blessed with lots of donors who send gifts of $100 or more in response to your mailings, then the cost-benefit ratio tips in favor of more elaborate and expensive packages, particularly the use of postage and personalization.

With that in mind, what are some things you can do to avoid hairsplitting traps:

1) Use white offset paper or a standard cream offset stock (and in almost all cases, using recycled paper doesn't cost anymore and helps our environment). Besides costing more, most colored stock or glossy papers make it more difficult to read your letters.

2) Use standard sized envelopes. Yes, the firm I work with uses lots of odd-sized and oversize envelopes when mailing for our clients, but only when we're mailing in large quantity or have been able to "gang" several projects together. The big disadvantage of non-standard envelopes is that they may fail to meet postal criteria or require additional postage.

3) Forget about using brochures or other inserts. Development staff and executive directors can spend weeks agonizing over the text and design of brochures or inserts. But in most cases these enclosures actually depress response. In direct mail fundraising, the letter is the workhorse of persuasion.

4) Don't offer premiums for acquiring new members. The purpose of direct mail fundraising is to provide a convenient way for enlightened and generous individuals to support causes and endeavors they believe in. In some instances, offering a premium lowers the response rate. Ill will is often created as well since many organizations have a dickens of time sending out premiums in a timely manner.

5) Discontinue the use of business reply envelopes. For your best donors, you can put a postage stamp on the reply envelope, but for almost all your other donors and prospective donors, letting them pay the postage doesn't decrease response and may in

fact increase response.

6) Use black ink — and use other ink colors sparingly. When using two colors, you can hardly ever go wrong with dark blue for the signature and the organization's logo (i.e. letterhead). Of course, the text of the letter should be in black. Any other color combination is hard to read (especially for older adults), reduces comprehension, and increases the cost of your mailing.

7) Don't worry about the alignment of your teaser. In fact, don't worry about teasers at all. Hardly any of the tests we've conducted for dozens of clients show that the addition of a teaser increases response. And it's so easy to be too clever. Stick with your organization's logo (unless it is too elaborate) and the "typed" name of the person signing the letter.

8) Save space and reduce confusion by *not* offering the option of making credit card gifts. Mailings whose reply devices have a line for credit card gifts often get lower response rates. Big DISCLAIMER: credit cards are helpful if you're inviting your members or donors to participate in a monthly giving program. And many individuals seem to prefer using their credit cards in responding to telephone fundraising and when signing up for special events.

9) Have your executive director or president sign the letter. Don't spend time trying to recruit a celebrity or worrying about which member of the board should sign. Members and donors expect the chief executive officer to know what's going on, to care about the organization, and to be responsible enough to ask them to send a gift. For variety's sake, in the course of a year, you may wish to have another staff member, board member, or other volunteer sign the letter, as long as they don't edit your drafts to death.

10) Do spend more time and more money on your thank-you letters and notes, as long as you don't delay in getting them out.

Don't try to save money by sending out your thanks via bulk mail. And don't send out post cards.

Thank you letters are a lovely place to include inserts to keep your members and donors better informed. And I guarantee you don't need to test, or split hairs, over the value of hand-written thank you notes to those who make generous gifts.

3.

Teaser Copy

Most teasers are about as useful as an 8-track tape – without an 8-track player. That's because a lot of organizations keep forgetting how intelligent and sophisticated donors are. If they've heard about your organization or if your organization's name sounds like something they're interested in, then donors open your envelope. Absent those factors, no amount of screaming or no degree of cuteness will save your package from the recycling bin.

Of course, there are exceptions.

A truly creative or brilliant teaser – one tied forcefully to the central concept in the letter – can sometimes work well. That's especially the case if there is a true crisis or emergency about your appeal.

Another important exception has been borne out by tests we've done for some of our clients. Membership or annual renewal notices appear to generate a higher response when the renewal process is telegraphed on the outer envelope. For example: "2003 Annual Membership: Please respond within 10 days" or "A reminder about your membership."

But most of the tests I've been involved with have shown that teasers, at best, don't improve response and, often, they *depress* it.

The U.S. Postal Service "Household Diary Study" suggests some of the reasons that teasers are less than effective in fund-raising mailings. It's "familiarity with the organization" that tips the scales when a recipient is trying to decide whether to open a piece of mail — or to toss it.

That's why we have much better experience with simply using the organization's name and address as the "corner card" in the upper left. We frequently put the letter signer's name and title — in Courier typewriter font — either above or below the organization's name and address: "John Albright, President."

We find that this simple format works well even for acquisition or prospect mail.

In most cases, a teaser telegraphs the reader that this mailing is "mass mail." Readers, according to the postal study (and confirmed by many focus groups), are most interested in mail that promises *useful* information.

When they are effective, teasers intrigue the recipient or promise a very direct, tangible benefit. Teasers also work when used as part of a membership renewal series (for example, "But too many organizations try too hard to be intriguing, and end up being trite, way too cute, or, more often, simply confusing). And, for most nonprofits, tangible benefits are difficult to offer.

4.

Soliciting Too Often

Most organizations send too many solicitations. In fact, with many of the groups I work with, we have been *reducing* the amount of fundraising mail every donor receives each year.

However, if you'll permit me a seeming contradiction, most organizations do need to increase the number of *mailings* they send out each year.

The reality is that the overwhelming majority of your members or donors are going to make *only one gift a year* to your organization. In most cases, that gift will be less than $100.

Thus, it's just not cost effective to send a special appeal every month to these folks. Two mailings a year should suffice: an annual renewal mailing (sent out in the first quarter of the year or in the anniversary month of their first gift) and the year-end appeal.

But there are a significant number of donors who want to make multiple gifts. They *enjoy* sending more than one check a year. In fact, because they value your organization, they want to increase their overall support, and the best way for them to do that is to send you several checks per year.

The most loyal of these donors will sign up for *monthly giving programs* — ideally, asking you to have funds transferred electronically from their bank accounts or having their credit cards charged each month.

Then, there is the one to five percent of any direct mail membership or donor base that is capable of and willing to make larger contributions. And these larger gifts really make a difference. Every $250 gift equals 10 of your typical $25 gifts, and it takes 20 $50 gifts to equal one $1000 contribution! However, getting these larger gifts almost always involves several mailings that include personalization, extra postage, and more expensive stock.

Of course, the real challenge is to find out which donors should receive only two mailings a year, and which ones want to receive multiple mailings, or which ones should be sent expensive, personalized mailings asking for larger gifts.

This means doing a comprehensive analysis of your database. You'll need to identify those who consistently make only one gift of less than $100 a year, and those who have on several occasions sent gifts of $100. This latter group should receive at least a couple mailings a year that are highly personalized, ask for gifts of $250 or more, and use a live postage stamp on the reply envelope.

Also, those donors who just joined your organization should, in general, receive several special appeals during the first year of their membership.

Beyond these specialized appeals, most organizations need to *send more informational mailings.* Newsletters should go out at least four times a year. An annual report is essential in many cases. Older donors or those who have been giving for many years should receive two, three, or four planned giving mailings a year.

Many organizations also find their donors appreciate receiving a Holiday Card that also thanks the donors for their generosity. A variation used by some is a greeting sent to donors at Thanksgiving time.

Further, an emergency situation or a spectacular accomplishment may warrant mailing a special report to all of your donors.

So, you probably aren't sending out enough mailings — at least not the right kind. Many of your donors really want to hear more about the wonderful work you're doing with the contributions they're sending.

5.

Welcoming New Donors

Welcome packages are a very good idea. If at all possible, please start sending them to those who make their first gifts to your organization.

Unfortunately, I don't know of a systematic study that tests *not* welcoming new donors against welcome packets. But we do see higher renewal rates for those clients with a full-fledged thank-you program than for those groups that send no thank-yous, who use post cards, or who send out late thank-yous.

And many of us have heard directly from donors about how they appreciate thank yous, and how they feel about those organizations that fail to acknowledge their gifts.

Finally, some of the organizations I work with derive significant revenue in response to the thank-yous and welcome packets they send - more than enough revenue to offset the cost of the acknowledgment program.

With regard to new members or first-time donors, my preference is to send out two mailings: a regular thank-you note or letter as quickly as possible, followed by a welcome packet a week or so later.

I also believe strongly it's a big mistake (and probably more costly in the long run) to send out thank-yous or welcome letters via bulk mail. Too often organizations wait until they get enough thank-yous to send this way - to save, really, just a couple hundred dollars (or even a couple thousand dollars) all year long. First class postage. It was practically invented for thank-yous. Use it!

What to include in your welcome package?

Several of the groups I work with have a special "Member's Guide" or welcome brochure that thanks the donor, explains any benefits, introduces briefly the organization's main programs, and lets the donor know how to contact the organization for more information.

At our firm, we also strongly encourage our clients to give all new donors or members a response card they can use to a) prevent their name from being exchanged, b) limit the number of special appeal mailings they receive, and c) request not to be telephoned for contributions.

Of course, a reply envelope should be included in any welcome packet - so that a new member may communicate with you or even send an additional gift.

Whatever you do, it's a good idea to have a cover letter for your welcome packet. State that you're pleased the donor has joined your organization and that you're grateful for his or her support. Let them know you'd welcome having them become more involved or request more information if they wish.

You'll want to think about including at least two other items - and maybe as many as six additional items. Here are some possibilities:

• Low-key planned giving brochure, preferably about charitable bequests

• Form or brochure that enables donors to make memorial or tribute gifts

• A directory of key staff people, with job responsibilities and phone numbers

• A list or mini-catalogue of publications available from your organization

• Brochure or flier about your monthly giving or sustainer program

• A bookmark designed especially for your organization

• Your most recent newsletter

• A survey about a donor's preferences or about his or her views on issues key to your organization

For most organizations, only 30 to 40 percent of those who make a first-time contribution ever go on to repeat their giving. But of those donors who do make that second gift, 60 to 80 percent go on to make many additional gifts - contributing hundreds and thousands of dollars. So any effort you make to welcome and involve new donors will make a great difference.

6.

Securing Donor Loyalty

Acquiring donors or new members is an increasingly difficult and expensive necessity. So anyone involved in direct mail fundraising is wise to ask how you can most effectively retain new members.

Here are 10 suggestions for building donor loyalty:

1) Send a thank-you as soon as possible after the gift is received. Put your thank-you in an envelope (no post cards, please) and send it via first class mail (don't wait until you get enough thank-yous to send them bulk mail).

2) A few weeks later, send a New Member or Welcome Packet. A warm and friendly letter (it can be printed) should welcome the new member, thank him or her again, and express a willingness to answer any questions or provide more information.

Possible enclosures for this welcome packet are your most recent newsletter, a planned giving brochure, a membership card, a listing of staff members and their phone extensions, and a catalog of your publications or resource materials.

Many organizations also give new members a chance to express their desire *not* to have their name exchanged, receive telephone fundraising calls, or get special appeal mailings.

3) Six to 12 weeks after you receive a first gift, invite the new member to become a monthly donor — including the opportunity to make gifts via credit card or electronic funds transfer. Newly acquired members often appreciate the opportunity to have their membership renewed automatically as monthly donors.

4) Be sure to include any new donors in special appeals or "house mailings" you send. New members will appreciate the additional information about your organization's special programs and emerging projects. (Of course, if a new member has requested not to receive special appeals, omit the person from these appeals).

5) If you don't have a newsletter (or magazine), start one. Keep your donors informed — even if all you send is a one-page "President's Letter" or "Director's Update."

6) I'm a big fan of annual reports because they're another opportunity to communicate with donors. They also fulfill the expressed desire of many donors who say they'd like more information about how their gifts are being used. Annual reports are also ideal vehicles for recognizing donors who are giving higher levels of support.

7) I also encourage many organizations to send holiday or Christmas cards to their newer members and their active members. (I know a couple of groups that send out Thanksgiving cards to beat the rush of holiday greetings.)

Holiday cards are a perfect way to say thank you to your donors for a year of generous support. If you're not fond of cards, send a year-end thank-you note. Many organizations include a "soft ask" (along with a reply device and reply envelope) in these holiday greetings.

8) Establish a series of membership renewal mailings (or annual fund mailings if you don't have members). Many donors won't get around to sending you a gift unless you tell them "It's time to renew your membership" or "We're counting on your annual gift again this year."

It's helpful to tell your members when they made their last gift and the amount they gave (and encourage them to give more). You'll need to send second, third, and fourth reminders to those who fail to respond to the first renewal notice — since some members won't send a gift until it's really clear that their membership is "lapsed" or "expired."

9) Inevitably, most of your newly acquired donors will fail to make a second gift to your organization. Don't be discouraged; that's part of the cycle of fund raising. Be prepared, though, to send out reactivation or "We miss you!" mailings to those who haven't made a gift for 18 months or more.

10) Finally, when you don't hear from members for a couple of years, include them in your acquisition or prospect mailings. This group of former members is almost sure to be the most responsive to your acquisition mailing. For some reason, many donors appreciate the chance to "rejoin" an organization. And then you'll have another chance to welcome and cultivate them so that they can become your most loyal and generous friends.

7.

Year-End Mailings

For many organizations, the year-end mailing generates far and away the most revenue of any single mailing. So this is the one mailing where you'll want to invest the greatest amount of your time and fundraising resources.

In fact, most of the organizations we work with send out *two* year-end mailings: the first in early November and a second in early December. Typically, almost all of those on a membership or donor file receive the first mailing while the second is sent only to the most generous and responsive of donors.

Whether you send one or two mailings, this is the time of year to make sure to mail something to all of your active donors, your recently lapsed donors, and if possible your former donors. In other words, this should be one of your largest donor mailings (or house appeals) of the year.

This is also the time of year to spend more money on your package. I strongly recommend that all active $100-plus donors and all frequent donors receive reply envelopes with first-class stamps already affixed.

For higher-level donors, create a separate segment of your mailing. Use a closed-face outer envelope — perhaps even hand-addressed. First-class commemorative stamps are most effective during this time of year as we sort our "business mail" while looking for those sought-after holiday cards from friends and families.

Your top donors ($100-plus or at least $250-plus) should receive personalized letters and reply devices. Mentioning the month(s) of their most recent gift(s) and thanking them for those gifts can be highly effective. If possible, the signer of the letter — your director, president, or chair — should hand-sign the letters to the highest level donors and add a hand-written P.S.

For everyone else, a pre-printed letter with a reply device and reply envelope in a window outer envelope is a cost-effective solution. Of course, if you have a small donor base (under 2,000 or 3,000), this is the time of year to gather a group of volunteers and send personalized letters to everyone.

What to say in these year-end letters?

Thank the donors for their loyal, faithful, and generous support. Let them know what a difference their contributions have made. Most likely, you wouldn't have been able to stay in business — or carry out a specific project — if it hadn't been for these wonderfully generous friends.

After you've thanked the donors, let them know you hope they'll make another contribution — a special gift — before the end of the year.

Then take some time to report to your members or donors what you view as your major accomplishments of the past year. Mention again how their support played a key role in these successes. In some instances, you may want to tell stories about individuals or families you served or who benefited from your organization's work.

Your letter can then go on to outline your plans for next year. What's ahead for the organization your donors care so much about?

Ask your donors to invest in these new projects or major directions. Encourage them to give now — before the end of the year — so that you can start at the beginning of next year with the strongest possible programs.

If you choose to send out two mailings, the second mailing to your responsive, generous donors can be very brief. Thank them again for their exceptional generosity and encourage them — "if you haven't already" — to send a gift before December 31. Wish them the very best for the holidays or, if appropriate for your donor or your organization, convey the religious significance of the Christmas season.

On the reply device of your year-end appeal, you may want to include a statement that your organization welcomes gifts of appreciated stocks and securities, which may result in significant tax savings. Certainly if it's the case, state that "Contributions are tax-deductible."

And, if you've forgotten all year to include your name, address, and phone number on your reply devices, shame on you! But this is the mailing to redeem yourself. What if someone loses the reply envelope — or wants to call you about donating a thousand shares of Microsoft?

8.

Monthly Giving Programs

Monthly giving programs are the financial backbone of many nonprofit organizations. An effective monthly giving program allows donors to select from one of three options:

1) Authorizing a monthly gift amount to be transferred to your organization from the donor's bank account.

2) Authorizing your organization to charge a contribution to the donor's credit card each month.

3) Sending you a check each month in response to reminders you mail to the donor.

As you can see, monthly giving programs provide a convenient service to donors who want to support your organization but feel they can send only small amounts. Giving monthly gifts is a way every donor can become a major donor: 12 gifts of just $15 add up to $180 each year.

Moreover, monthly donors remain loyal and are excellent prospects for charitable bequests and other planned gifts.

Best of all, monthly giving programs are quite efficient. The cost of raising each dollar is very low. That's especially true if most of the monthly gifts are being made by electronic funds transfer or via credit card.

As wonderful as these programs are, they're not for every organization.

If you're diligent and also have responsive donors, perhaps you'll persuade five to 10 percent of your donors or members to become monthly donors. More likely, it will be just one or two percent. So you'll need a donor base large enough to justify the cost of setting up and getting a monthly giving program. In most cases, that means at least a donor base of 5,000.

And because getting a monthly donor program to a profitable level of support is very time-consuming and expensive (it will take several years before you reap the real rewards), you'll need to make a genuine organization-wide commitment to this endeavor.

The best way to get started is to interview or even visit at least two or three organizations with monthly programs in place. You should also talk to those vendors or businesses that process credit card transactions and electronic funds transfer for nonprofit organizations.

You'll also need to devote at least a significant portion of one person's staff time to overseeing the program.

Once you've done your homework, consider these suggestions:

1) Come up with a special name for monthly givers. But don't make it sound so onerous or serious that no one will give. "Guaranteed Giving" would be a turn off. My favorite is "Guardians of the Lake," used by a well-known California environmental organization.

2) Send out an invitation letter to all those donors whose highest gift ever is less than $50 and who have made at least two con-

tributions. You'll need to spell out any special benefits or recognition you offer monthly donors.

3) Regularly invite all new donors to join your monthly giving program. Include articles about monthly giving in your newsletter. In your membership renewal mailings, offer a monthly giving option (including automatic renewal).

4) If your donor base is big enough, asking donors by telephone to put their monthly gifts on credit cards is the most effective technique for building a monthly giving program.

And once you've enrolled monthly donors, don't forget about them. From time to time, send them special thank you notes and even modest thank you gifts. These monthly givers are sure to become your most productive and dependable source of revenue, and they'll respond enthusiastically both to information about your organization and to your expressions of thanks.

9.

The Value of Thank You Letters

If you've ever thought about saving money by eliminating thank-you letters, drum that notion from your head.

Donors are the most valuable resource your organization has. They act with extraordinary grace and exceptional generosity. You should come to your office every day eager to write thank you notes. And making phone calls to thank your supporters should be among your most favorite activities.

In fact, your best donors should receive *additional* thank you notes from the executive director or president. A board member should send a third note. And it wouldn't hurt for a program staff person to send a letter of appreciation as well.

Most donors don't hear often enough from the organizations they support - except when they receive appeals. Thank you letters are a wonderful opportunity for you to communicate with your donors. Indeed, your letters should encourage them to communicate with you as well - by encouraging them to visit, call, or write back with comments and suggestions.

I'm convinced, in fact, that one reason individuals send gifts is because they were thanked for their previous gifts. They sense their contributions are appreciated and so they repeat this positive behavior.

10.

Guidelines for Effective Tests

As testing is the golden gateway to increasing your effectiveness, keep the following suggestions in mind:

First, test only items or factors that make a real difference. In other words, what you test is as important as how you test.

The savvy fundraiser will test whether *spending more money* is the best way to raise lots more money. As the experienced development director and consummate consultant Jane Breyer often says, "Your job in development is to raise money – not cut costs."

The best place to raise more money by spending more money is to test whether first class postage outpulls nonprofit postage. An even better test – but done carefully – is whether a "live" first class stamp on the return envelope generates enough additional income to offset the extra cost. In most cases with current donors or members, it does. Finally, with regard to postage, if you're using business reply envelopes, test "Place Stamp Here" reply envelopes. In the course of the year, you'll save lots of money in return postage.

Speaking of spending more money, you may want to test having more personalization in your packages. Instead of a "Dear Friend" letter, you can have a letter "laser personalized" to each individual donor with the appropriate salutation. It can be very effective to cite – with effusive gratitude – the individual's most recent gift. You can also ask the donor to consider a gift of a specific amount (calculated on the individual's giving history).

An aspect of this personalization test would be to have the individual's name and address lasered or inkjetted on what is called a closed-face envelope (as opposed to a window envelope). Don't, though, apply a label to a closed-face envelope.

As you can imagine, all of this personalization is expensive, especially because all the pieces need to match up. But with certain donors and with certain organizations, this additional investment can more than pay for itself.

Another important test – one that can save money *and* boost response – is to leave out any brochures or other inserts in your mailings. Often these expensive items distract your donors or members from the all-important message in your letter.

You also might want to test whether you can get by with a two-page letter – as opposed to the four-page letter – when you're sending out mailings to recruit new members or acquire new donors. Typically, the longer the letter the better the response, but there have been cases where the shorter letter works as well – and, of course, costs less.

Don't be tempted into testing trivial matters – like ink colors or subtle changes in the size of the package. What you test has to have the potential to save lots of money or make a big difference in response.

Once you've decided what you want to test, then it's essential that you do follow strict procedures for testing. Only by following *specific* guidelines can you produce dependable test results. So please take time to read one or more of many helpful books available, including the volume by Mal Warwick, *Testing, Testing, 1, 2, 3: Raising More Money with Direct Mail Tests*. To summarize the key steps you'll need to take:

1) Test *only one* thing. You can't test a colored stock and first class postage because you won't know whether it was the color or the postage that made the difference.

2) You must create panels to test against each other: one will be the "control" and the other will be the "test." These panels are created by *randomly* selecting donors and splitting them into two (or more) equal groups.

3) Test panels must be large enough – have enough records or names in them – to generate meaningful response. If you have a control of 2000 and a test panel of 2000, and you generate 30 and 20 responses respectively, you don't have enough information to draw valid conclusions. As a rule of thumb, I like to have test panels of 30,000 each (a total of at least 60,000) for mailings to acquire new donors – and at least 5,000 in panels for appeals to current donors or members.

4) Make sure your test panels mail from the same location on the same day.

5) Don't draw conclusions from statistically insignificant results. In other words, the difference in results (response) between the "control package" and the "test package" has to be great enough to suggest that, if you repeated this test, you'd come out with similar results. What's involved here is "confidence level," and most mailers prefer at least 90 percent. There are formulas and "confidence tables" in *Testing, Testing 1, 2, 3* and in most other books. But even a quick look will tell you that 320 responses

against 300 responses doesn't make the first package a sure winner.

6) So the last guideline is to re-test. Certainly you want to repeat a test if the results are statistically significant, but you also want to repeat tests because donor attitudes and behavior do change over time. It is also the case that as your organization grows and matures, certain factors may be more or less important in persuading individuals to respond to your mailings. What worked -- or didn't work — three years ago may be old hat by now. Testing, then, is a powerful tool for keeping your mailings fresh and your fundraising effective.

11.

Donors' Attitude Toward Mail

If you surveyed people, you'd find that hardly anyone eats fast food or watches much commercial TV. And almost no one likes direct mail. Most certainly they hate telephone fundraising calls.

I guess that means those of us involved in development work have a lot more free time – which we can spend preparing gourmet meals and watching only public television.

Seriously, if you receive a phone call or a letter from a donor asking to receive less mail or to be removed from your mailing list, you should absolutely respect those wishes. In fact, at my firm we help organizations design welcome and thank-you mailings that give donors some options to reduce the amount of mail and phone calls they receive.

But the reality is, if you don't mail often to your donors or members, *and* ask them to make a gift, then more of your supporters will lapse. In part, they lapse because they move and you don't receive their forwarding addresses. But, just as importantly, if you mail only once or twice a year, you'll be appealing to many of your donors at a time when they don't have time or money, or both, to send you a gift.

We've found, too, that a donor's attitude toward mail changes from time to time. If your donor is really busy, not feeling well, or getting lots of mail from other groups, he or she may get angry and say they don't want any more mail. But in some cases, after several years, we've written or phoned those who had asked not to be mailed or phoned and they confess surprise that the organization was told not to contact them.

So, what to do? We urge you to take what we believe is a more respectful and sophisticated approach. Be honest and tell all donors or members that they will receive at least a year-end appeal in addition to their annual renewal mailing – because the organization wishes to keep them informed and involved in supporting a cause they clearly care about. Then donors are encouraged to let the organization know if they wish *not* to receive appeals and phone calls beyond these two mailings.

In most cases, we also urge organizations to send their newsletter to every donor and to send thank yous in response to all gifts – even if a donor says, "Don't bother to thank me."

Newsletters and thank yous are important bonding tools for direct mail and should only be set aside when individual donors insist on it.

12.

Telemarketing to Lapsed Donors

While telemarketing has proliferated -- as have the complaints -- it still can be an effective way to reactivate your lapsed donors.

What else can you do, after all? Just give up on those donors? Send them more mailings? You've already sent them mailings and they haven't responded.

If you sent an invitation to your very good friends – most of whom are busy with many demanding responsibilities – and they didn't respond, what would you do? Write them off for good? Wouldn't you give them a call and find out how they're doing?

All of us get too much mail, and many of us can't keep track of our charitable commitments. It's an especially big challenge because so many of the organizations we care about send us confusing mailings – with print that's so small we can barely read it along with tiny photos that don't make any sense.

Lots of organizations ask us to use our credit card to contribute, so we set the letters aside since it takes time to find the right card, fill out all those pesky numbers, and then sign our lives away.

Besides, it's partly your fault that some of these donors are lapsed. Your thank-you letter didn't go out quickly enough. Or perhaps you just sent a post card to acknowledge their gift. And you didn't get around to getting out a newsletter for a couple of months. Or a mailing came back with "address unknown" and you didn't take the time to call to get that new address.

So, unless you're prepared to spend a lot more money on acquisition mailings (and we know how peeved nonprofit boards get about that expense!), you would be wise to plan on at least one re-activation phone program a year.

Of course, you'll want to hire a reputable company, one that works with *nonprofit* organizations (commercial telemarketing is very different from charitable calling). You'll also need to comply with any state charity requirements since telephone calls are highly regulated.

You'll also need to have enough lapsed donors to make the phone call cost-effective (and you should carefully review the list to make sure foundations, board members, or major donors aren't called). If you don't have a couple thousand names, it probably makes sense to send out a "final notice" mailing.

But if you have enough names and if you use a professional telephone firm, then calling your lapsed donors will give you valuable information. You'll gain some useful insights into why people have let their support lapse. You'll also get news about specific donors – the death of a spouse, retirement, or other changes in their circumstances. On a more positive note, some donors will ask to be sent more information about your organization or about planned giving.

Calling your lapsed members will also provide you with the key that unlocks future giving: *updated and corrected addresses.* One of the primary reasons donors "lapse" is that they no longer receive your mail — they've moved or you have an incorrect address for them. (You're able to reach them *by phone* because they've kept the same number or their phone number has been found through an electronic matching service.)

The majority of organizations we work with derive huge benefits from the careful yet consistent use of telephone calls to their donors. And a sizeable percentage of those donors express appreciation that a phone call helps them stay connected and involved with causes they care about.

Those organizations succeed, in large part, because the executive director and development staff have learned to set aside their "pet peeves." If you want to raise money and if you want to respect the donors who contribute that money, your own likes and dislikes have to take a back seat to what works.

13.

Last Gasp Renewal Strategies

If you have a number of lapsed donors or members to whom you've sent six or seven appeals but still they don't respond, here are a few "last gasp" steps you can take to attempt to reactivate these individuals:

1) Be sure to let your readers know the *date of their last gift*. You can even say, "I'm concerned that we haven't heard from you since your generous gift in December 2002."

When surveyed, donors say the primary reason they haven't renewed is that they didn't realize it had been so long since their last gift. In a poll of lapsed members for one organization we work with, an overwhelming majority indicated (mistakenly!) that they'd made a gift within the last 12 months.

2) If you have a newsletter or magazine, let your lapsed donors know you'll have to discontinue sending it to them. You might consider a P.S. in the letter and a tick box on the reply device: "I'm unable to send a gift at this time, but would like to continue to receive the newsletter."

3) Stamp FINAL NOTICE or LAST REMINDER on the outside envelope. It's a good idea to include Address Service Requested on at least this notice, so you'll get back information about those who have moved.

4) Have the response device be a *brief survey* about why the individual is choosing not to renew support. The accompanying letter should thank the donors for past generosity and acknowledge that there are valid reasons why individuals change their giving. You'll get useful information from this survey, but you'll also find that a sizeable percentage sends along gifts.

5) A variation of the above is to send a letter that recognizes that the donor has ceased giving. *Don't* include a reply device. Rather, the letter invites the lapsed member or donor to *call* or *e-mail* the person signing the letter (best case: the executive director or president – lapsed giving is a serious matter for your organization!). Indicate that the donor may also jot a brief note.

Do include a reply envelope. This technique is more expensive since it "demands" a closed-face, typed or laser-address outer envelope, but it can reap large rewards of both information and giving.

6) For those who have given $50 or more or for those who have been donors for a number of years, it can be effective to send a handwritten note with an outer envelope that has been hand-addressed. Including a stamped reply envelope gets the best results.

This is a lot of work, but perhaps you have some volunteers who would take on this project. There are also companies that will do it for you. The time and expense involved are worth it. These handwritten notes generate two to four times the response of normal renewal notices.

7) If it's been 18 – or perhaps 24 months – since a donor's last contribution, then it's time to include that name in your next mailing to acquire or recruit new donors or members. In effect, that individual is no longer a donor, but rather a prospect who must be re-educated and re-inspired to join and make a "first" contribution to your organization.

These acquisition mailings are typically much less expensive than donor mailings, so they are a very cost-effective way to re-activate lapsed donors.

14.

The 'Last Mailing Unless We Hear from You ...'

Some mail order catalogues include the following announcement: "Unless we hear from you, this will be the last correspondence you receive from us." Will a similar warning from your organization get results? Not likely.

Your appeals and mailings are designed to activate your donors' philanthropic values and beliefs. Charitable giving is voluntary; there's no law that says people have to give to your organization, and a donor shouldn't receive any significant tangible reward for her contribution. So not hearing from you isn't any big loss to a lapsed donor.

Besides, it's almost never cost-effective to stop sending mailings to your long-lapsed donors or members. To be sure, you shouldn't be sending them expensive newsletters or even mailing to them that often. But they should regularly receive acquisition mailings until they again become donors, and sending inexpensive re-activation mailings once or twice a year will often generate net revenue – and help keep your donor base from shrinking.

The primary reason donors let their giving lapse is *not* that they cease to care about the issue you address or that they're unhappy with your organization. In mailing after mailing, in telephone calls to lapsed donors, and in surveys, lapsed donors admit they didn't realize how long it has been since their last gift.

Other reasons that donors lapse include retirement, changed economic circumstances, and moving out of a nonprofit's service area. Indeed, we often find that those members who are lapsed have undeliverable addresses or phone numbers no longer in service. It's hard to elicit gifts from donor when they can't receive your mailings.

From a fundraising management perspective, another reason donors lapse is that they aren't receiving enough mailings from your organization. For example, a donor makes an initial gift in January, doesn't get a thank you letter until mid-February, the first newsletter is delayed until April, and then there isn't another request for a gift until the year-end appeal in December. If the donor is busy or not feeling flush, then the chance of keeping that donor active through giving is very, very slim.

That's why I strongly recommend that nearly every organization – whether it has members or donors – have an annual renewal program that includes at least four mailings. Mailings two through four go to those who don't respond to the first renewal.

In those annual renewal (or annual fund) mailings – as well as in re-activation mailings to long-lapsed donors – the most effective fundraising technique is to let the individual know the date of their last gift. One way to phrase that is, "According to our records, your last gift was 19 months ago, in April 2001. If we've overlooked a recent gift, please let us know."

Don't give up on your lapsed members and donors. And take steps now to keep your current donors from becoming lapsed by sending them more information and providing them more opportunities to support your organization.

15.

Most Common Mistake

Mailings for which I'm responsible, as well as the mailings I've observed, run into trouble when the four key elements of direct mail fundraising — list, gift request, package, and copy — aren't properly balanced. These four elements must be appropriate to one another and coordinated in a way to achieve your objectives for a specific mailing.

For example, if you're mailing to a list of 10,000 people who've never given to you before — *and* you request a gift of $500 *and* you send out a slick, four-color package using first-class postage *and* your one-page letter is filled with lots of insider jargon — then your mailing is almost sure to fail.

Direct mail fundraising is literally a balancing act, whether you're writing to current donors or potential donors.

Take the former case. If you're mailing to a *list* of your top 100 donors, then you should in most instances *ask* for substantial contributions based on their giving history. The *package* should use lots of personalization and be printed on attractive paper stock; postage should be first-class and the reply envelope should have a first-class stamp attached. Further, the *copy* should be friendly and personal, with lots of gratitude for their generous support in the past.

On the other hand, acquisition mailings to prospects need to use a lighter, more economical touch. Spending lots of money almost never raises the response rate enough to justify the additional costs involved.

One big difference is that acquisition letters tend to be longer, usually four pages. Letters to your best donors should in some cases be longer, especially when you're launching a new program or undertaking an important initiative. However, with your donors, one or two-page letters are often effective.

Acquisition letters are typically printed in just two colors on lightweight stock, without personalization, and using only two sheets of paper (with text printed on both sides).

Another way to describe the fundamental flaw I see in much of direct mail fundraising is the failure to tailor the mailing to the specific audience you're addressing. My sense is that an organization becomes so involved and passionate about its cause or its program that it forgets to communicate appropriately with its donors and prospects, with the different levels of involvement and interest that characterize these varied audiences.

16.

Conventional Wisdom that's Wrong

Here are three pieces of conventional wisdom about direct mail fundraising that are flat-out wrong:

• Long letters outpull short letters.

More and more, we're finding that you can use short, one-page letters to acquire new donors or members. But it's very, very important that you test these shorter letters against longer letters. From a creative standpoint, your short letter should draw attention to itself as a brief letter. And any year-long plan for appeals to current donors should include some brief letters.

• Always try to get your donors to upgrade their gifts.

The terrible truth is that very few donors will ever send a contribution larger than their initial gift. In fact, many donors send subsequent gifts that are at a lower dollar level (fortunately, a meaningful percentage will give at higher levels). But, it's a big mistake to use every appeal to ask donors to give larger gifts. Some — if not the majority — of your appeals should ask donors to match their last gift or give at the same level.

• Always include a reply envelope.

Your best donors support you financially not because they're "donors" but because they care about your organization, the people you serve, and the issues you address. So, treat them like friends and — at least once a year — send a mailing just to thank your most responsive donors for their generosity and involvement. It's also appropriate to send letters that only present important information — letters that don't ask for a response and that don't include a response envelope.

17.

Raising Money on the Internet

Overscheduled and over-committed as you probably are, should you invest time and resources in raising money on the Internet?

In a word, no. But you should give someone in your organization the responsibility for making sure there's a full-featured website up and running, one that provides basic information about your organization and describes the work you do.

Web sites have become like newsletters (in fact, they are electronic newsletters). They don't raise a lot of money but they're essential in providing the context and credibility for your fundraising activities.

Today, any organization without a Web site (and e-mail address) will give pause to prospective donors. You'll need to have cyberspace credentials if your organization is to be taken seriously.

I'm sure, too, at some more distant point, electronic communication will either replace direct mail entirely as we know it or become an equal partner with paper communication. When that day arrives, fundraisers will post their appeals on the Web (or its successor) — and then wait to count the credits that appear in their electronic income accounts.

But the good news about being a development professional is that you can wait until everyone else adopts new technology — and gets all the bugs worked out. In other words, you don't really need to worry about being behind the curve.

By its very nature, philanthropy is "old fashioned." It reflects core values passed down from generation to generation, and there are certain rituals (like writing checks and mailing them off in response to letters that are "typed" in Courier) that change more slowly than society at large.

So my recommendation is, that you continue to improve your skills in traditional — yet evolving — forms of direct mail fund-raising. Those skills will help you communicate more effectively with your present donors, and the same principles of communication that undergird direct mail will certainly strengthen electronic fund raising when it's time for you to make the switch.

18.

Nurturing Your Donors

There's a lot of talk these days about nurturing the donors you have – rather than spending an undue amount of time and effort on acquiring new donors.

But the truth is you will still need to spend lots of time and effort (and money) on recruiting new donors or members for your organization. A robust acquisition program is *more than a necessity* – it's an opportunity to strengthen your entire development program.

With an influx of new donors, you'll increase and regulate your organization's cash flow, and you'll be creating new prospects for charitable bequests and planned gifts. Perhaps, best of all, you'll be giving more people the chance to become involved in your organization's programs or its issues.

Those new members and your current members do need to be nurtured. What's important is to be clear about who these people are; they aren't everybody on your mailing list. As always, you want to select those to be nurtured based on the recency of their gift (someone who gave 19 months ago isn't a current donor), the dollar amount of their gift(s), and the total number of gifts.

Here's a baker's dozen of ideas for nurturing your wonderful donors:

1) Speed up the turn-around time and expand the content of your thank yous.

2) Make phone calls to donors who send gifts of $500 or more (or $250-plus if you can manage it). Leaving voice mail messages is fine.

3) Offer the convenience of monthly giving – especially through electronic funds transfer and credit card transactions.

4) Make sure you have a newsletter and that it goes out at least four times a year.

5) Lapel pins with your logos are inexpensive – a lovely expression of thanks for all those donors who give $100 or more.

6) Use your annual report to recognize donors whose annual giving is above $500.

7) Establish giving societies to recognize annual giving (and lifetime giving if your organization is old enough) – with a display of those names in your organization's lobby or conference room.

8) Whenever you send a mailing to your current donors to request an additional gift, make sure that – early on in the letter — you also thank them for their past generosity.

9) If you exchange your mailing list with other organizations, offer your donors an opportunity to be excluded from those exchanges.

10) Send a year-end Christmas or holiday card to your current donors – or, if you want to try something different – a Thanksgiv-

ing or a New Year's greeting.

11) Ask board members to send an additional thank you note to your best donors.

12) Offer your members or donors a chance to receive *periodic* e-mail updates.

13) Try to send at least one mailing a year *without a reply device or reply envelope* – just send a letter that thanks these donors for their financial support and provides information about a new project or your organization's progress.

19.

How Many Mailings Per Year?

If your organization raises money through the mail, you face a fundamental dilemma: if you don't send enough mailings in the course of a year, you'll experience higher than desired levels of donor attrition. But, if you send too many mailings some donors are certain to complain about "too much mail."

The reality, though, is that you must send out *at least four letters* – winter, spring, summer, and fall – to almost everyone who has given a gift within the last two years. Any fewer and you're wasting your organization's money and your own time. Typically, this would work out to one mailing in late January, a second in April or May, a third in July or August, and a fourth in November.

Ideally, you'd also send out at least one – if not two or three – very personalized appeals to those who have given $100 or more. These wonderful individuals deserve a special opportunity to make even more generous gifts to your organization. You may even wish to establish giving clubs or societies to encourage ever increasing annual support.

It's also the case that you can't have a direct mail program unless you're willing to send out a *newsletter* to your donors or members. Again, I'd recommend at least four issues. These newsletters don't need to be elaborate. Four issues of a four-page newsletter are much better than two issues of 16 pages. Most donors or members want a quick overview of how their contributions are being used.

So we're up to eight mailings, perhaps nine or more if you can send specialized mailings to $100 and over donors. This mailing schedule represents the *minimum* of what you'll find cost-effective.

But let me take it a step further. You'll actually be able to raise more net revenue if you can send out *three separate mailings in the fall*: one in September-October, another in early November, and a final reminder and thank you to your most responsive donors in early December.

And, you'll also find that adding a *membership renewal series* or an annual fund appeal will generate a lot of contributions and boost donor retention.

In the course of a year, current members or donors should also receive one or more mailings that *don't* ask for money. The best examples are those that encourage legacy giving or charitable bequests. An annual report without a request for a gift might also be appropriate as a mailing to your more generous donors. And some organizations send a Thanksgiving or holiday card to express appreciation to donors.

If you add up all these suggestions, you'll easily be sending out at least one mailing per month and possibly as many as 24 mailings in a 12-month period. To be sure, any single individual will likely receive 12 or fewer mailings (see Part III for suggestions about targeting and segmentation). It's also essential that you diligently honor requests from individuals who ask to receive fewer mailings or only one mailing a year.

Yes, this is a lot of mailings. But if you set up a schedule – and stick to it – you'll find that you'll raise more money and will retain more of your donors. Direct mail fundraising works best when you give your donors enough opportunities throughout the year to support the organization they care about.

II.

ACQUIRING AND RENEWING DONORS

Direct mail serves as the foundation of many successful fundraising programs because it generates annual revenue, identifies prospects for major gifts, and leads eventually to charitable bequests. What's more, these results are predictable.

But another predictable aspect of direct mail fundraising is that some donors will *stop* giving to you. They move away, they lose interest in your organization, their income changes, or their health deteriorates.

You simply cannot sustain a direct mail fundraising program unless you're consistently investing in efforts to acquire new donors. And if you want your program to grow – and reap the rewards of more cost-effective mailings because of *decreased unit costs* – then you'll really need to get serious about acquiring new donors.

The best way to acquire donors or members is through acquisition or prospect mailings. Typically sent out in large volumes, these acquisition mailings use combined lists from several different organizations and publications.

There is a real science to selecting these lists, and list brokers make a living doing just that. But whether you rely on a list broker or do everything yourself, you should understand the basics of selecting prospect lists.

In the pages that follow, you'll also find tips about how to create an effective acquisition mailing – and how to sidestep some of the mistakes that can cause costs to skyrocket and response to plummet.

This part of *Open Immediately!* also offers suggestions to help you hold on to those newly acquired donors. Often the way in which you acquired donors will dictate special care in how you seek that all-important second gift – and a life-time of giving.

As with so much else in direct mail, you should be suspicious of your own intuitions and avoid taking too big of a risk. As you acquire and renew donors, depend more than ever on the touchstone of effective direct mail fundraising: test and test again.

20.

The Need to Continuously Acquire Donors

At every organization, some level of donor attrition is inevitable: people die, others move away. In any given year, at least 10 percent and more likely 20 percent of your donor base will fade away.

If you stop acquiring donors now, in as few as five years you could end up with next to none. Therefore any organization desiring a long-term future must invest in some level of acquisition.

A second reason for continuously acquiring donors or members is that they're the most likely to become monthly donors. If invited by mail and, especially by telephone, a meaningful percentage of these individuals will agree to authorize their bank or credit card company to send you monthly gifts. A strong monthly giving program is the best way to generate predictable and high levels of net income you can use to fund projects and programs.

A third reason to keep in mind is that direct mail fundraising is more cost-effective as the quantities of your mailings increase. The per unit cost for a 5000-piece mailing is much higher than for a 10,000-piece mailing. Printing, mailing, and postage costs are all lower on a per-donor level. That means your mailings will produce more *net* income.

In sum, if at all possible send out acquisition mailings at least three times a year. Ideally, four or five times. If you have only one acquisition mailing per year, you increase the odds it won't succeed. Conversely, with several mailings you spread out the cost and risk.

Perhaps the biggest advantage to sending out several smaller acquisition mailings (not too small, though) rather than one large mailing is that you'll be more likely to send out thank-you letters promptly. Getting too many new donors at one time can create a backlog for data entry staff, and your renewal rates will diminish as a result.

21.

Testing Variables

The most important factor to test in your first acquisition mailing is whether or not direct mail is even a feasible way for your organization to enlist new donors or members. And to best answer this question, you'll need to mail at least 30,000 pieces — and preferably 50,000 to 60,000. Better yet, 100,000 pieces or more.

In your initial test mailing, you should test various types of lists to see which ones will work best for you. This way, you'll get a reading of future potential.

Generally, these lists should be the ones you feel are most likely to do well. But you should also test lists with larger donor universes, and non-donor files, too, such as magazine subscribers. This way, you'll be more likely to have "roll-out" potential for future acquisition mailings.

Usually 5,000 is the minimum number of names needed to test an individual list. Thus, a 50,000-piece mailing will let you test 10 different lists.

It's almost always essential to merge-purge your lists. A merge-purge won't just reduce your costs (by lowering the duplication rate). It will also help ensure that results aren't "polluted" by duplicates or existing donors.

Restrict your *first* mailing to just one package, unless you're mailing in larger quantities. This will keep your design, printing, and postage costs to a minimum.

And remember: The *real* test is whether or not direct mail will work for your group. To maximize the chances that you can make it work for you, spend time — and money — to secure the best possible lists, the most persuasive text for your letter, and the strongest possible visual design. Lift letters, buckslips, decals, or stamps should be considered. With the best package as your first effort, in future mailings you can test to see what corners can be cut.

Copywriter Bill Jayme said it well: "I believe in going for broke. If I were launching a new venture, I'd pack everything into the initial package. And then, if the package was successful, I'd test down ... cutting back on costs until returns began to hurt. If you start with an economy package and it bombs, you'll always wonder what would have happened if you had gone for broke in the first place."

22.

Declining Response Rates

For many groups, response rates to prospect mailings are faring worse than in years past. What's more, in the past 20 years, average gifts in response to prospect or acquisition mailings haven't increased.

Despite these trends, there are still lots of exceptions. Some groups are actually getting higher rates of response to their acquisition mailings. A few are even bringing in enough gifts from new donors that income exceeds the cost of the mailing.

In most cases, this happens with a new, exciting organization mailing for the first time. Or there may be a lot of media attention on the issue or problem addressed by the organization. But, in general, response rates are lower.

There are important factors behind this trend. Let me try to explain.

One of the secrets of direct mail fundraising is that, especially in the "golden days of direct mail" (any time before the last couple of years), many of the "new donors" were actually individuals who were already donors or members. Many organizations didn't bother with the merge-purge process — in particular they didn't eliminate their current donors from lists they were mailing — and, as a result, thousands of these donors slipped through the cracks and were counted as new donors.

In recent years, almost every organization has their prospect lists "merge-purged" because this process also includes postal presorting and bar-coding to achieve the maximum postal savings. This has also meant that overall response rates are lower.

The second key factor is that most organizations no longer rent or exchange donors or members who contribute $50 or more (or $100 or more). The result is that the best prospects are no longer on the lists used for acquisition purposes.

A third factor in reducing response to acquisition mailings has been the tremendous increase in the number of Direct Marketing Association "preference" names — those individuals who have written to the DMA to request they not receive prospect mailings. We've seen some mailing lists with 15 percent of the donors or members coded "DMA Preference." Three to five percent is typical. Most reputable organizations respect those wishes and don't send them their acquisition mailings.

In my view, it's a great mistake then to conclude that "Direct mail doesn't work anymore" or "People are sick and tired of all that junk mail." In general, more Americans are giving in response to direct mail — and they're using direct mail to buy clothes, make investments, and carry out hundreds of other transactions.

But what should you do if *your* organization isn't attracting as many new donors as in the past? Here are some suggestions:

1) Plan to *invest more* in acquiring new members or donors. I know it's hard to convince boards and executive directors to keep spending more money to get fewer new members. But if you don't make that investment, then you will acquire ever fewer donors

and eventually your database will wither away because of inevitable attrition.

2) Step up your efforts to renew and reactivate your current members — fight the natural tendency of donors and members to fade away. Add a reminder notice to your renewal or annual fund series. Use a live-stamp reply envelope in at least one of your renewal mailings. Send special mailings to let your donors know it's been some time since their last gift.

3) Lavish attention on new donors or members. In a competitive environment, these wonderful individuals have chosen to support your organization. Aren't you lucky? Let those new donors or members know how grateful you are. Beef up your thank-you letters to these new donors, send them packets of information to welcome them as new members, and try calling to thank them for their gifts.

Even though prospect mailings cost a lot more and even though response rates are challenging, the good news is that 30 to 50 percent of those new donors will go on to make a second gift. A few of the groups I work with are seeing even 55 percent. And their average gifts will be much higher than their initial gifts. That's what continues to make direct mail such an effective fundraising tool.

23.

High Response, Low Renewal

There is some truth to the generalization that lists which pull unusually well often deliver donors who are hard to renew. The corollary seems to be true as well: lists with low response rates help you acquire donors who renew at higher rates.

But don't worry a lot about this – and certainly don't let it keep you from sending out acquisition mailings. Unless yours' is a large organization that sends out millions of pieces a year, these factors aren't terribly important.

What is important is that you try to acquire as many new donors or members as possible. And to do that, you'll need to expand your tolerance with regard to response rates, which can vary from half of one percent to as high as two percent (but not very often that high!).

In an ongoing acquisition program, you'll need to test new lists all the time – and most of them won't work well. You'll also find that some lists will work well for a while, and then suddenly fall off.

But if you keep mailing – and keep learning from your tests – you'll find some lists that will be very responsive, and these will maintain the momentum. They'll add lots of donors to your database and gifts to your income chart. And enough of these donors will make second gifts, and many of them will over time increase their level of giving.

The more we research the results our clients are achieving, the more convinced I've become that new donors – acquired at almost any response rate or at any cost – eventually repay the investment made to recruit them. The challenge is to make that investment as cost-effective as possible – but also as large as possible so you can acquire as many new donors as possible.

Worry less about response rates in acquisition and more about how to boost the response rate of your renewal or resolicitation mailings. And, while you're at it, take another look at your thank you letters or acknowledgements. Getting those out promptly and with effusive thanks will have the biggest impact on renewal rates.

24.

How Important are Response Rates?

Especially at the start of a donor or membership acquisition program, you shouldn't be driven by arbitrary standards of response rate or average gift. Rather, you should be sending out mailings that represent the true work of your organization.

With good writing (usually by an experienced copywriter), a faithful picture can be presented in a readable and engaging way. Such a presentation should portray the value of your work for your community or the larger society. And your letter should make clear why the reader's financial support is both urgent and essential.

Then you have to send out your mailing, hold your breath, and wait. You'll soon find out how many individuals are willing to support *your* efforts, and what level of contribution those new donors feel *your* organization is worthy of receiving. In a year to 18 months, you'll also learn how many of those new donors will renew their support and how many will increase their contributions.

At that point, you'll be ready for what will probably be a difficult discussion with your agency's financial manager and, in many cases, your board of directors. Namely, how much you will invest to acquire new donors *at a rate sufficient to replace attrition* or loss of donors.

Eventually, you'll have several cycles of direct mail acquisition and renewal behind you. Ideally, you'll have examined some of the checks you received, read correspondence (including complaints) from donors, and made phone calls to say "thanks" when a gift arrives.

In the process, you'll discover that most of those who support you have high levels of income. They probably are also well-educated and avid readers (even though they usually give a cursory reading to your mailings).

But that's not why they're sending gifts to you. If that were the case, you could simply rent lists of high-income families. Or lists of college graduates or magazine subscribers.

Rather, your donors give because *they care* about the issues you address or the people you serve. And how much they care relative to their other interests and concerns – along with how well they perceive you do your work – affects how large a gift they send. The result is that many wealthy individuals will send you only modest contributions. However, some middle-income families will send contributions of $100, $500, or even $1000 because they believe so strongly in what you do.

That's why, when acquiring new donors, you should give highest priority to renting and exchanging lists with organizations most like yours. And asking for gifts of $15, $20, or $25 – with exceptions in each direction – will help you acquire the most new donors or members.

Striving for high average *initial* gifts in direct mail is a fool's errand. Better to rejoice when those exceptional new donors increase their giving as they learn more about the wonderful work you do.

25.

Repeat Mailings to Responsive Lists

One of the terrible truths of fundraising is that, almost always, a mailing list doesn't pull as well the second and third time you use it. That decrease in response rate (and sometimes in average gift) is true whether you're using all or part of a list. And it's true whether it's a subscriber list or a donor list or a membership list.

But still it can be profitable to *re-mail* a list as often as three or four times a year.

Even with a three-percent response (quite high for an acquisition mailing), there are theoretically 97 percent left who might respond. For many potential donors, hearing from your organization repeatedly may prompt them to make that initial gift. Remember, too, that some lists, such as subscriber lists, will be updated with new names at least twice a year, so if you re-mail to a popular list you'll be reaching some new people.

A final note: do monitor whether these newly acquired donors renew or repeat their support 12 months from now. In some instances, lists with very high response rates have very low renewal rates.

26.

Multi-Buyers on Rented Lists

When you do a merge-purge on the lists you rent, you'll notice a sizable number of people who appear on several lists - duplicates, if you will.

Often these so-called merged dupes or multi-buyers (using the lingo of catalog mailers) work very well. After all, these are individuals who like to respond by direct mail.

You have the right to re-mail to these names, but tread with caution.

For some of the organizations we work with, it's not worth mailing them a second time or third time: the response rates are well below the average responses for the mailing as a whole.

Here's how to find out how your organization should use your duplicate prospect names:

The first way (the cheapest and fastest) is to print about 15 percent more packages than your projected mail quantity. Or if you're well organized, wait to order your print quantity until after the merge purge and see precisely how many duplicates you have. Then three to four weeks after you drop your acquisition mailing, send exactly the same package to your merged duplicates or multi-buyers.

If you get promising results (typically, we expect the response rate of duplicates to rank about in the middle of other prospect lists), then you can try a more expensive and time-consuming strategy: add the word "reminder" to the outer envelope and perhaps even a smaller-sized "follow-up" note to the package.

In most cases, it's *not* effective to try the third approach of creating an entirely new and different package to send to the merged duplicates. The cost of designing and printing a new package isn't offset by a higher response.

It's also been my experience that sending out a third and fourth mailing to duplicates works only in exceptional situations. There are relatively fewer names to mail, and the additional lettershop costs are much greater than any income you might derive from a third or fourth mailing.

27.

Donors Usually Renew at the Same Level

Those of us who write the letters and select the mailing lists have only a limited impact on the person's level of interest and the amount of discretionary income they're willing to send as a contribution. We can suggest gift amounts, but what makes this *philanthropy* is that the donor ultimately decides what amount to send.

In fact, you'd probably be surprised to learn that some of your big gifts come from individuals who aren't wealthy but care a lot about what you do. On the other hand, you receive $25 and $50 gifts from millionaires. Even more to the point, that same millionaire may make $100,000 gifts to another organization – but, unfortunately, not to you.

In contrast to this unpredictable variability in gift amounts is the other reality about direct mail: people's giving levels are based on habit and thus very predictable.

Most of us have too much to do and too much information to assimilate. As a result, we simplify our lives by doing what we've done in the past. In fact, we even make a virtue out of this; we strive to be consistent in our behavior because we've learned that most people don't really like surprises.

These habits – especially those relating to philanthropic behavior – are often learned early in life and operate at a subconscious level.

This is why it's so hard to persuade the overwhelming majority of donors to give larger gift amounts. But you shouldn't quit trying. You may want to suggest very modest increases of just $5 or $10 if they typically give $25. Or you should certainly encourage donors to make small gifts each month – the ultimate in a consistent habit!

28.

Big Givers Likelier to Renew

In most cases, individuals make larger gifts because they have more disposable or discretionary income – or believe they do.

But the reasons these higher level donors renew at a higher rate are complex. In the first instance, whenever you select a subset of a whole (say, donors whose highest gift is $100 and who have given in the past 12 months), you create a more responsive segment. Statisticians can explain it in a way I can't, but my hunch is that the names and addresses of the subset are more accurate than those across the entire database.

Second, donors who give higher initial gifts tend to get better thank you letters, and often their subsequent mailings are more personalized. This special treatment will encourage a higher percentage to renew their support.

But whatever the reasons, the important consequence of this reality is that these new donors really are more valuable to your organization. Around my firm, we've started saying to each other, "$100 donors rule." They're always a relatively small percentage of a donor database, but their generous and continuous gifts stand out in any individual mailing – and their impact on annual income is immense.

The best way to keep acquiring these $100+ donors is *not* to devise acquisition mailings that target supposedly wealthy individuals. Nor should your acquisition or prospect mailings ask only for gifts of $100 or more. Rather if you carry out an ongoing acquisition program (with three or more mailings spread out across the calendar) and if you keep testing new and different lists, you'll inevitably acquire more and more of these wonderful donors.

29.

Retaining Your Donors

Acquiring new donors is expensive and time-consuming ... but absolutely necessary. To get the most out of your investment in acquisition, you must carefully track your retention of new donors by asking:

1) Of the donors acquired this year, what percentage can be expected to make a second gift?

2) How many of these repeat donors are likely to support you for years? And,

3) What is the best renewal program for achieving these numbers?

Our experience is that only 40 to 60 percent of those who become new donors to your organization will make a second gift.

Of the 40 to 60 percent who do make second gifts, 60 to 80 percent will keep giving for some time. And, *on average*, these repeating donors will give amounts larger than their initial gifts. I say on average because almost all donors keep giving the *same* amount as their *initial* gift (or even less), but a precious few will substantially increase their giving.

The moral of this story about percentages is *not* that you should sit around and moan about the high cost of direct mail fundraising.

Rather, you should take steps to make sure *your organization's* percentages are as high as possible, and to encourage donors to increase their giving levels.

The first and most important step, in this regard, is to send out a prompt thank-you to every new donor. If possible, send out a welcome package or kit (see Part I). In addition, really smart fund raisers place telephone calls to thank new donors, especially those who make initial gifts of $100, $500, or $1,000 in response to mailings.

There is a more direct answer to the third question, namely, how to structure a renewal program to keep the largest possible number of donors giving to your organization.

Almost every organization will benefit from an annual renewal or membership renewal program. For small organizations, every-one - new and old donors alike - should receive their renewal notices at the same time every year. One of our environmental clients, for example, has their annual membership renewal on Earth Day each year.

For bigger organizations (more than 10,000 or 20,000 names) sending out renewal notices on the *anniversary month of a donor's first gift* keeps retention rates high — although it's a lot more work, more expensive, and requires computer savvy.

Whether you follow an annual renewal or anniversary renewal cycle, the key to success is to have a *series* of reminder notices - at the *very* minimum three, but more likely five or six. Organizations that retain a high number of members send out 10 or more.

In other words, renewal notices are sent out to everyone on your database, with the exception of those who have made very recent or very large gifts. (You can, if you wish, use the first renewal letter to say thank you again to these wonderful donors). Then four or five weeks later, you send out a second mailing - a reminder notice, if you will - to those who didn't respond to the first mailing. And so on through four or five mailings.

As part of a renewal program, many organizations find it effective to place *phone calls* to those who haven't yet responded to the renewal mailings - giving them one more opportunity to keep their membership status alive.

We've found it's most effective if you treat these donors as "members." This works even if you don't have a formal membership structure. If you're unable to call your donors members, at least call them friends as in "The Friends of Melrose Hospital."

The message should be kept simple. In the first notice: "It's time to renew your annual support as a Friend of Melrose Community Hospital." Be sure to thank them for their support in the past year ... describe *briefly* what you accomplished with their support ... and suggest what their continued support will achieve in the months ahead.

Subsequent notices should indicate that you haven't yet heard from them about their annual membership support. Urge them to renew as quickly as possible. Your final notice should indicate that their membership has lapsed - but that you don't want to lose them as members and that they can still reactivate their membership by sending a gift today.

You'll achieve the greatest success if you plan these renewal efforts as one, inter-linked series of mailings. You'll also be able to print some elements at the same time and thus save yourself money. Then stick to the mailing schedule and you'll be much more likely to renew over half of your new donors and retain a very high percentage of your continuing donors.

30.

Donors Acquired with Coffee Mugs and Other Premiums

Whether or not to use premiums involves an evaluation of all your efforts to acquire new donors and to renew those donors. First, there's an important distinction when it comes to premiums:

Front-end premiums are those included with the mailing that requests a contribution. Calendars, greeting cards, name stickers, and decals are currently among the most popular front-end premiums.

Back-end premiums are those items promised to donors and prospective donors after a gift (usually of a specific amount or level of giving) has been received. Books, tote bags, videos, coffee cups, and umbrellas are all used frequently as back-end premiums.

Both types of premiums are used to acquire donors — to get prospects to make that initial contribution to your organization. The use of premiums sometimes increases response rates and sometimes (although less frequently) boosts average gifts. In our experience, it's not so much that individuals are contributing simply to get a premium. Rather, it's because front-end premiums encourage lower-dollar initial gifts. And donors who make lower-level gifts are statistically less likely to make a second gift, and those that do continue to give at a lower level.

Thus, even though premiums may boost response and revenue at the front-end (and there are very valid reasons for doing that), you should plan on lower renewal rates from donors or members acquired in those mailings.

What's more, you must test whether the use of premiums actually increases either response rates or revenue. For some organizations, premiums do exactly that. But for many others, premiums — either front-end or back-end — haven't tested ahead of non-premium mailings. It appears that premiums work best when used by organizations with high name recognition or very broad-based appeal.

Finally, when considering whether to use premiums, economies of scale play a pivotal role. To effectively use front-end premiums like calendars and name stickers, you must send out at least a few hundred thousand pieces. Half a million or million — or tens of millions as some of the very large organizations do — make those note cards and decals much more cost effective. And, if you use back-end premiums, you need a large enough quantity of responses to make it time and cost efficient.

What all this means is that, if you're thinking about using premiums, be sure to talk with other organizations that are using them in their mailings. And plan on working with those printers and mailers who specialize in these premium packages. You'll get the best prices and you'll avoid postal problems.

31.

Renewing Donors Acquired by Premiums

What's the most effective way of renewing donors acquired by using premiums? Use a premium again.

But be very careful about the premiums you select if you wish to stay on the good side of the post office.

This caution applies to the use of "back-end premiums" — those items you send donors *after* they've sent a contribution of a certain amount. If you're not careful, your mailings will be considered "advertising" and the premium to be a "product." And then you won't be able to mail at nonprofit postal rates.

The more typical challenge for nonprofit organizations is when they've sent a "front-end premium" — calendars, greeting cards, name stickers, and other items along with the letter seeking a contribution.

As I said in the previous chapter, donors acquired through these front-end premiums often renew at a lower percentage rate than donors acquired without premiums.

One of the ways to boost the renewal rate for premium-acquired donors is to improve your thank-you program. Make sure all new members or donors promptly receive a thank you letter or note. And send along an insert — your latest newsletter, a news clip, or even a simple "program summary." By including more information in your thank you, you'll help your premium-acquired donors understand the good work you're doing.

When it comes time to send a renewal or special appeal letter to your premium-acquired donors, you'll find it helpful to suppress or omit those donors who gave less than $10. In most cases, you won't get back enough money to offset the cost of mailing to them — unless you're mailing in very large quantities.

Your letter should attempt to let the donor know what a gift of a specific amount will do. For example: "Your special gift of $50 provides the seeds and tools that will make it possible for an entire village to plant a grove of trees." In this way, the impact of the gift — the result the contribution makes possible — becomes, in effect a "premium" for the donor.

A technique effective with all donors is especially helpful in trying to renew donors acquired with premiums. Either in your letter or on the reply device, indicate the amount of the donor's last gift and the date of that gift. Ask the donor to help out again — perhaps by doubling the amount of gift.

Finally, you'll need to be prepared to put the majority of your premium-acquired donors back into your acquisition or prospect mailings. Many of those who make initial gifts in response to premium mailings will make very small initial gifts, and the majority of those responding won't send second gifts even after receiving renewal mailings or special appeals during the 12 months following their first gift. So the best strategy is to send these non-responding donors another acquisition mailing. They'll almost certainly respond at a much higher rate than the other prospect names you mail.

III.

TARGETING YOUR MAILINGS

As we saw in Part One, direct mail fundraising works so effectively because it connects your organization's mission with individuals who care deeply about the values and beliefs reflected in that mission. The challenge, then, is to target your mailings so you reach the right audience with the right message and the most effective gift request.

Part Two discussed how, when you're acquiring new donors or members, you can successfully target lists of individuals who are the most likely to be interested in your organization.

When you send mailings to those who are already your donors, you target your appeals through *segmentation*. Breaking up your mailing list into groups of donors (or segments) allows you to use your organization's scarce resources to invest money in mailings to those who are most likely to respond – and to encourage them to increase their giving.

Besides saving money, wise segmentation can also help prevent donor attrition. And carefully planned segmentations, consistently implemented, are essential if you wish to track results to your mailings. By studying those results, you're able to refine your segmentations – and adjust the sequence and scheduling of your mailings – to achieve even better results in the future.

In addition to segmenting your donor list, you should target the look and content of your appeals to reflect an understanding of the heart and mind of your donors.

Once someone has moved from being a prospect to becoming an actual donor, he or she joins a community of shared values and beliefs, people who have expressed their ideals and commitments in tangible financial support.

If you have the resources, focus groups can help you discover what your donors are thinking and what motivates them to give. But every professional fundraiser will want to talk with donors on the phone, read letters and notes from them, and research the demographics of those who contribute in response to direct mail.

Understanding your donors and then targeting your mailings will enable you to raise even more money now and retain donors who will give to you in the future.

32.

Why People Respond to Fundraising Letters

One of my continuing concerns is that those of us in fundraising don't know our donors or members well enough. That's why I'm a big advocate of calling to thank people when they send in a gift – it's the best way to find out why they're supporting your organization.

I also encourage people to spend some time processing gifts: opening envelopes, looking at the checks, reading the notes or comments often sent along with the gifts, and noticing which mailings are generating lots of responses.

Too, organizations can benefit from a more extensive survey or poll of their donors to find out who they are and why they give. Ideally, this research would also involve either focus groups or longer interviews with several donors. These more free-form conversations add insights to the more numerically based analysis.

With that as background, here's my stab at the 10 reasons people respond to fundraising mailings:

1) They are thanked – both in response to their last contribution and in the appeal letter itself, which early on should express

gratitude for the individual's generous support.

2) They are asked. In other words, the letter makes it clear that this isn't an essay or a report but an explicit request for a contribution at this time.

3) They trust you will put their gifts to good use. In previous mailings and publications (newsletters, annual reports) and in the letter you're sending now, you demonstrate that you're operating in a diligent and effective manner.

4) They share core values and beliefs with your organization – what you do is accomplishing a greater good.

5) They want to get something done or they like solving problems. Your letter either reflects a determination to get the job done or you show how practical and achievable your solution is.

6) They're angry or upset about something. Sending a gift becomes a way to express outrage or to protest an action or behavior the donors believe needs exposure.

7) They feel compelled to respond to an emergency or a crisis. They're pleased your group is dealing with an urgent situation and see their gifts as a way to make a difference.

8) They appreciate the information and insights you provide, including those in your newsy, chatty appeal letters. Individuals who respond to direct mail are overwhelmingly well educated and are avid readers. They've learned that if they contribute to organizations, they get news about achievements and challenges.

9) They would like there to be a public record of their support. It's hardly ever the primary or only reason donors send gifts, but many do like others to know they support your cause or organization, which is why listing donors in your annual report or

newsletter can be so effective.

10) They're loyal to your organization and want to maintain their personal tradition of contributing to you. That's why membership renewal, annual fund, and re-activation mailings have very high rates of return.

Even though I believe every one of these reasons for giving motivates some of your donors some of the time, I do realize that – at some level – both we and the donors themselves can't really explain rationally or systematically why we write checks when we receive direct mail appeals.

There is a certain mysterious and irrational quality to philanthropy. In one sense, the reason that some people respond generously to direct mail is that they are part of that wonderful segment of the population that does just that.

So be sure to give your donors many opportunities throughout the year to do what they enjoy doing: send gifts to you. And be as effusive and appreciative as possible when you send thank you letters to these extraordinary individuals.

33.

Finding Out about Your Donors

If you're writing a letter to your donors or members, you must know who they are — what percentage are women or men, as well as the number of married people and your donors' age.

How do you find out this information? First of all, your database should be able to give you regular reports on gender and marital status.

Secondly, if you're going to be writing fund raising letters, you should spend several days a year — at different times of the year — processing incoming mail. There's nothing quite so instructive as looking at the actual checks, seeing where people live, noting who signs the checks, and judging how young a person is from the way the check is signed. You'll also get to read all the wonderful comments and notes that donors send along with their contributions.

Third, the effectiveness of your entire fundraising program will increase significantly if you survey your members or donors. The best way to get statistically valid information is to conduct a five-to ten-minute telephone poll of a random sample of 1,500 to 2,500 names in your membership or donor database.

Once you have a better sense of who your donors are, how should that influence the way you write your appeals?

I am wary of the generalization that 75 percent of all checks to charity come from women (usually the statement is "women over 50"). But there is some value in the conclusion that's often made because of this generalization: namely, write a letter that is more heartfelt, more emotional, more personal.

Indeed, my own test of a good fundraising letter is whether it's a letter I'd write to my own mom.

But I think the prescription to write an emotional and personal letter has less to do with gender and more to do with philanthropy. Another way to state the matter is that an appeal to our charitable impulse is an effort to touch the "feminine" dimension in all of us.

Even more importantly, effective fundraising letters are about people — and about the values and beliefs that move people to take out their checkbooks and mail off charitable contributions.

So take time to find out who your donors or members are — and then write letters with language that speaks to their values and beliefs, not their gender.

34.

Using Focus Groups

Focus groups can be an effective way to strengthen and expand your direct mail fundraising program. And if you have the budget to invest in this useful research medium, here are three guidelines worth considering:

1) Hire a marketing consultant or market research firm that has a track record in conducting focus groups. They'll be able to handle the logistics, arrange for the meeting place, and conduct the actual group interview so that you derive the maximum amount of useful information. Yes, that will cost you at least $5,000 and perhaps as much as $25,000, but it's worth it.

2) Plan on having several focus groups. Don't rely on just one group session. If possible, have different groups in different cities if you're a national or regional organization. Have groups of donors and non-donors. Perhaps have sessions in two different times of the month. From this variety of groups may emerge some common themes, or you may learn that different audiences respond to different messages or approaches.

3) Remember, the results of focus groups are not statistically valid. This is *soft* research. The information you gain will be impressionistic and the insights will be suggestive. You'll need to spend time digesting the information and exploring how what you learned relates to your direct mail program. So don't count on the focus groups to give you fast and sure-fire "fixes" for overhauling your direct mail program.

You may want to consider "harder" or more statistically reliable research if you're trying to answer more specific questions. Telephone polling can quickly gather information from a random sample of your membership base.

Mailing out surveys is often less expensive but it takes longer to gather information, and repeated mailings are usually necessary to make sure the results have statistical confidence. By mailing out surveys, you do often get useful written comments and you do give your donors or members a sense of participation in setting your organization's direction.

35.

Baby Boomers as Donors

For fundraisers, the year 2000 was a watershed year because that's when the first Baby Boomer turned 55. Born between 1946-1964, Boomers are 77 million elephants our society is trying to digest.

We are the largest, richest, and most dominant group in American society. We built McDonalds and we're in the process of transforming so many other businesses and institutions. As has been the case throughout our lives, we will strive to be different from our parents.

But, as a direct mail fundraising professional, I'm still betting that the aging process will, as it has in the past, transform Boomers from consumers to philanthropists (most philanthropists — especially those who use direct mail — are 55 years and older).

Already, there is evidence from the Roper and Gallup polls that Boomers may be even more generous than their parents. By some calculations (especially average gift), they are already giving more. What are some of the reasons for my optimism?

1) Boomers are more likely to be college-educated — twice as

likely as their parents, in fact. College-educated Americans are better informed (National Public Radio and the New York Times national edition show how information-hungry Boomers are) and have more discretionary income — two important characteristics of direct mail donors.

2) Boomers are self-centered, some would say spoiled. After World War II, for the first time in history, wages were high enough that mothers could stay home to indulge children (who had fewer brothers and sisters to compete with). Direct mail and fundraising are perfect for individuals who wish to be communicated with personally and have a desire to express themselves.

3) Philanthropists are generous not just because they have high incomes but also because they have the sense of security that comes from assets (like stocks and real estate). Boomers are likely to inherit lots of money; their assets will be more than enough to sustain their busy lifestyles. Because of high wages, the real estate boom, and the stock market appreciation, the parents of Boomers are estimated to pass on at least $7 trillion.

But Boomers are different from their parents, so changes in approach are already being made in direct mail. We are always testing letter length because our hunch is that Boomers will want either shorter or longer letters. Providing a credit card option is also another important test to carry out on a regular basis (Boomers love credit cards!).

The most important way you can prepare your organization's direct mail program to appeal to Boomers is to increase the amount of information you gather about your donors. I strongly recommend focus groups, telephone polls, and targeted interviews to gather research both about your current donors and the next generation of donors.

You should also consider sending surveys to your donors or members — to get their views and wishes about your organization's work and how they'd like to be treated as donors.

Thank you letters should also provide an opportunity for your donors or members to let you know whether they wish to receive regular appeal letters (or hear from you only once a year) and telephone appeals. Many donors will also give you information about their first name (for salutations), birth dates, and other personal data that will help you treat them as individuals.

So in sum here's my view: as Baby Boomers age and as your organization learns more about them, you are certain to experience your own boom in fundraising.

36.

Guidelines for Segmenting

Who you send your fundraising letters to is what makes the biggest difference in the response you receive. The challenge, though, is that any system for selecting potential recipients — how you segment your donor or member file — can impose some dangerous "logical conclusions." In my experience, the dangerous dimension of segmentation strategies has prompted organizations to make one of two mistakes:

A) To mail without any segmentation at all, or

B) To construct a needlessly elaborate model for dividing up the file.

To avoid these mistakes, start by asking yourself two questions:

1) Does my segmentation model insure that my best donors (most gifts, highest previous gift, most recent gift) are getting the special treatment they deserve (first-class postage, personalization, live-stamp reply envelope)?

2) Is my mailing large enough to warrant a more sophisticated

segmentation model? If you're not mailing more than 5,000 names, don't worry about doing anything more than segmenting the very top portion of your donor file. You won't get enough extra response and upgraded gifts to offset the increased costs of printing, data processing, and lettershop charges involved in a complex segmentation.

If your donor base is large enough for more complex segmentation, the *recency of gift* is the key factor in predicting the response rate of most direct mail-acquired donors.

Thus the easiest way to reduce costs and boost response is to limit your mailings to those individuals who have made gifts *within the last 18 or 24 months*. After that point, there's almost always a significant fall-off in response rates.

Finally, don't confuse segmentation with keycodes or mail codes (sometimes called "stimulus codes" or "source codes"). Segmentation is about sending different packages to different sets of donors or members. Within segments — or even if you don't segment — you should try to imprint a keycode on each reply device or mailing label. Typically, there can be a dozen (and often more) different keycodes for each mailing.

These usually include numbers or letters to signify the specific mailing (e.g., your year-end appeal) and then a series of letters or numbers to represent time period of last gift, number of gifts, and the range of the highest gift.

Using keycodes or mail codes will help you track response to the mailing, indicate which group of donors or members are most responsive, and suggest how you might want to segment your mailings in the future.

37.

Creating
Usable Segments

Segmenting your database of donors is one of the most effective ways to generate higher rates of response, larger gifts, and more total income.

What it allows you to do is to make sure that your best donors receive better treatment – and that you don't spend too much time on the least responsive donors. As the father of modern management, Peter Drucker, puts it, "Feed the winners and starve the losers."

Large organizations (say with 50,000 or more donors) and commercial mailers can benefit from very *complex* segmentation models, ones using regression analysis and other sophisticated statistical tools. But to simplify matters here, you can create segments that reflect the following factors:

The most important variable in terms of whether a donor will make another gift to your organization is called *recency*. Donors are segmented by when they made their *last or most recent gifts*: typically, 0-6 months, 7-12 months, 13-18 months, and 19-24 months. After 24 months, donors are often segmented by years because, in most cases, someone who hasn't made a gift in over two years behaves much like someone who has never made a gift to your organization.

The second most important criteria in creating segments is the *amount* of the donor's highest previous gift (HPC), sometimes called highest gift ever. Statistically, a person who has once given you a gift of $1,000 is much more likely to make another gift than someone whose largest gift is just $10. Of course, lots more donors will give you $10 than will contribute $1000. But that's just the point: you want to spend more money mailing to $1,000 donors and less money to all those $10 donors. So you'll often see a database segmented by $0-9, $10-14, $15-24, $25-49, $50-99, $100-249, $250-499, $500-999, and $1000+.

The third factor in predicting donor response is the number of gifts an individual has made to your organization, usually called *frequency*. A donor who has made three or more gifts to your organization is much more likely to give again than someone who's given only once. As a result, organizations will often segment their donors by those who've made one gift, those who've made two gifts, those who've made three gifts, and those who have made four or more gifts.

If you take all these factors together – which you should – then those donors who have given a gift of $1,000 at some time, who have made a gift in the last six months, and with four or more gifts to your organization, constitute the most responsive (and generous) segment of your database. That will be a small segment, but those donors are the ones who will produce the bulk of your contributed income.

At the other end, individuals who made just one gift of $10 or more, two years ago, is a segment that should receive infrequent and inexpensive mailings.

How many segments and which of the three parameters you should use depends on the total size of your database. Having too many really small segments becomes meaningless at best – and expensive when it comes to printing, personalization, and lettershop. In most cases, you'll want to create segments that take into account all three factors – recency, frequency, and amount (called "RFM" by the experts).

As you try to do this with your own donor base, I can give you a technical clue: the easiest way to create these segments is to break the database into hundreds of cells defined by:

- The date of the donor's most recent gift,
- The amount of her highest gift, and
- The number of gifts made by the donor.

In a sense, then, these cells become the building blocks that are used to create larger segments. With this approach, an example of a segment would be: all donors whose most recent gift is 0-6 months, whose highest gift is between $25-49, and who made only a single gift to your agency.

Another segment could be based on the date of the donor's *first gift*, since those who have been with you the longest are more likely to stay with you. An example would be: all donors who have given since 1997, in the amounts of $25-49, and who have given at least two gifts annually.

Then, too, at some point in the course of your annual mailing program, you'll also want to segment by *cumulative giving*. In that mailing, you'll write to let the donor know that "So far this year, you've generously contributed a total of $500. I hope you'll consider matching that support with a special gift at this time."

Segmentation is one of the most complicated aspects of direct mail fundraising. It's sometimes tempting to make it too complicated, but I would urge you to work with your colleague to develop a system that's appropriate both for the size of your donor base and for the range of mailings you send in the course of the year.

Spending time on segmentation will produce huge dividends for your organization.

38.

Donors, Not Segments

Always keep in mind that you're not sending mail to segments, but to real people who care about your cause. We seem to lose sight of this in our strategy sessions or when we're tabulating responses. Here are a few suggestions to help keep you focused:

• Use a professional telephone fundraising firm to call and thank your donors. Monitor the calling. Read the caller comments.

• Survey your members to find out who they are, what they read, what they care about, which groups they support, and what they like about your organization.

• Hire a professional polling company to conduct a brief telephone survey. It can cost $5,000 to $25,000 but you can get a lot of reliable information very quickly.

• Hold focus group discussions of your donors, either on your own or, ideally, using a market research firm.

• Call a long-time donor just to chat. From time to time, visit donors if you can — and not just your major donors.

• Invite donors to visit your offices.

• Write personal notes on your thank-you letters. It will

remind you that you're writing to individuals.

• Read your letters out loud to the oldest, kindest member of your staff.

• And, finally, I'll share my own secret: I always imagine I'm writing a letter to my mother.

39.

Mailing to Low-Dollar Donors

At what dollar level does it become counter-productive to keep someone on your file? The answer is: as long as the cost of mailing to them is less than the amount of income you receive from them.

Certainly, though, you should limit the number of mailings you send in the course of the year to your smaller donors. Mailing to them twice a year, say in the summer and at year's end, may be plenty.

Another technique we've found helpful at my firm is to *include* donors whose gifts are $10 or less in acquisition or prospect mailings. These mailings are almost always larger and cheaper than any other ones you send out. And your "low-dollar donors" don't seem to mind using these mailings to fulfill their giving to your organization.

Membership renewal mailings, from my experience, also work quite well with these donors. Again, these mailings are usually less expensive than others. And they often have an upgrade encouraging some small donors to "get with the program" and become $25 members.

Even greater income may be derived from small gift donors, particularly if they give several gifts. They are ideal prospects for a monthly sustainer program and may be candidates for your planned giving program.

As you try to upgrade your current small donors, you might also include more tests in your acquisition mailings to try to get more donors to make higher first-time gifts.

Whatever you do, don't consign these donors to oblivion. If you decide to "take them off your file," be sure to archive the names and addresses to a tape, disk, or CD so that you or someone can retrieve them in the future.

40.

Calling Low-Dollar Donors

Unless you have about 10,000 small donors ($10 or less) and unless you ask them to become monthly donors via their credit cards or by electronic funds transfer from their checking accounts, calling these donors won't be cost-effective.

Even if you wanted to take the long-term view that upgrading a small percentage of these donors would be in your benefit, the odds are against you.

Remember, two of Hitchcock's "Terrible Truths" about fund raising:

1) The overwhelming majority of donors never give a gift greater than their first gift to an organization and,

2) Most donors downgrade rather than upgrade.

The good news, though, is that the very few donors who do upgrade do so significantly.

Therefore I suggest a more fruitful tactic: encouraging your $10 donors to give more than one gift a year — so that their cumulative giving does increase. A *monthly giving program* is the best vehicle for this. For those who prefer not to be monthly donors, an appeal that includes two or three reply devices (and reply envelopes) will make it easier for those donors to give multiple gifts.

Putting $10 donors in your acquisition mailings is also a cost-effective way to give them an opportunity to keep supporting you. Acquisition mailings are typically one-third to one-fifth the cost of an appeal to your current donors.

Still another way is to include a reply envelope in your news-letter — that could generate some gifts from your $10 donors (although the new accounting standards may upset this cost-effective fund raising strategy).

But please don't spend too much time or too much money trying to upgrade your $10 donors. Instead, devote your efforts, through testing, to find out how you get new donors to make an initial gift of $15 or more.

41.

Vendors as Donors

You should send letters to your organization's vendors — including reports about the wonderful work your organization is doing. In fact, send them thank you letters, even if they haven't given you a gift. Thank them for their support through the services and supplies they provide.

But don't spend a lot of time on vendor letters. Your results will almost certainly be disappointing (although the fundraiser in me is optimistic enough to believe you'll eventually get a delightfully surprising gift).

Remember, the purpose of direct mail is not to persuade people to like you, or even to convince them to give to you. Rather direct mail is targeted toward those 1) who already admire your work (or they admire organizations like yours), 2) who care deeply about the issues or problems you address, and 3) who already give to you or to similar causes. And, in most cases, that means individuals, not organizations or businesses.

Some of your vendors may well meet the first two requirements, but they're unlikely to meet the third qualification. In some cases, an owner or a staff person might be philanthropic and use the financial resources of the business to make a gift to you. But that will be the exception. And your letters should certainly be directed to that person.

So, don't ignore your vendors, but build your direct mail fund-raising program on more frequent and personalized communication with your current donors, and step up your efforts to reach out to more individuals who are most likely to contribute to your cause.

42.

Using Segmentation to Raise More Money

Yogi Berra is reputed to have said, "You can observe a lot by watching."

The first and perhaps most important use of segmentation is to help you evaluate the results of your mailings and the health of your donor or membership database.

Donors are typically assigned segments by aggregating groups of them based on:

• Their highest previous contribution ever (HPC or amount),

• The date of their most recent contribution (MRC or recency), and

• The number of gifts they've made to your organization (frequency).

Now the trick is to make sure the reply devices for your mailings have a key code (source code or stimulus code) that reflects both the specific mailing *and* the segment the donor belongs to. That way, you'll be able to produce reports showing which segments are most responsive to your mailings – and which segments produce the most revenue.

In general, the better segments (those with the highest previous gifts, the most recent gifts, and multiple contributions) will respond at a higher response rate than those segments where the donors have made only a single gift and made that contribution some time ago. If that's not the case, then there's something wrong with your mailing and probably with your segmentation model.

The purpose of all this tracking and evaluating is so that you can make the second most important use of segmentation: deciding which segments *not* to include in your mailings.

Over time, you'll begin to see that entire groups of donors should receive *fewer* mailings from you – perhaps only an annual fund or membership renewal mailing and a year-end appeal. Some segments may be so unresponsive that they should receive only acquisition mailings, which are inexpensive because they're mailed in large quantities.

The money you save by not sending all of your mailings to all of your donors can now be invested in spending *more money on your best segments*. That's the third use of segmentation: selecting those groups of donors whose response rates and average gifts warrant the use of first class postage (including the reply envelope), personalization in the letter and reply device, and higher quality paper. Typically, that's a segment of donors who have given more than $100, have given within the last year or so, and who have made multiple contributions to your organization.

The fourth way to use segmentation is to set the amount of money you want to request as a gift in your letter and on your reply device. Of course, you could ask each person to make an individualized gift based on his or her giving history. But that's often not cost-effective. It's also unnecessary because you'll find that the overwhelming majority of donors or members fall into clear categories of giving.

For example, there will be big groups whose highest contribution ever is $100 and there will be an even bigger group of those who regularly give $25. Especially for those segments where gifts are under $100, setting across the board gift requests for $100, $50, $35, and $__ can save you time and money. These gift amounts can be pre-printed on a reply card or imprinted by your lettershop or mail house.

If you've followed me this far, you've probably realized that the overarching purpose of segmentation is to keep your most active members or donors giving to your organization. And to encourage them to increase their giving or, at least, not decrease the level of their giving.

If executed carefully and consistently, segmentation in mailings will result in having donors "move up" from lower segments to higher segments. To be sure, many donors will "move down" – primarily by failing to make a second or third gift and thus they'll slip into the segment of lapsed or former donors.

But as long as you're acquiring new donors or new members – and you're sending out enough mailings with enough personalization to your best segments – then the top segments of your donor base will keep getting larger year after year.

IV.

WRITING EFFECTIVE LETTERS

Perhaps the greatest paradox of direct mail fundraising is that very, few people will ever read your letter (and almost no one will read every word). Yet a well-written letter is the single most important element in your fundraising package. Only in the rarest of cases can you use the mail to raise money without including a letter.

After reading the pages that follow, you will – I hope – realize that the place to start your letter is with your reader. In a real sense, writing an effective fundraising letter is an extension of the targeting we talked about in the last section. Writing to those who are already your donors or members requires a different approach from persuading those who have yet to make their first contribution.

Whether writing to generous long-time donors (and filling your letters with words of appreciation) or reaching out to prospects, your letter should ultimately be targeted to *one individual.*

Fundraising appeals work because they are personal, one-to-one communication. In the pages that follow, you'll find many suggestions for making your fundraising letters feel like an animated conversation with a good friend.

As strongly as I feel about writing easy-to-read, persuasive letters, I do hope this section will help you avoid spending too much time on the letter. Trying too hard to incorporate suggestions from every staff or board member is a formula for disaster.

To be sure, long letters sometimes outperform short letters, but saying too much and aiming for perfect clarity will sap your letters of the personal, friendly quality that make them effective fundraising tools. Save the time and effort so you can get out more letters to more donors.

43.

Seven Deadly Sins of Letter Writing

The *first* and most crippling flaw I see in so many letters is the tendency to write essays, rather than personal letters. When I'm drafting a letter, I'm always imagining a single donor or prospective donor, often someone I actually know. I try to "talk" with that person — carry on, if you will, an imaginary conversation — about why they might want to make a gift.

The *second* quality that deadens many fund raising letters is a style that's too stiff and formal. Fundraising letters should be chatty and friendly. To be sure, you can cross the line and presume a degree of intimacy that is inappropriate. But at the very least strive to use first and second person (I and you) and informal language (contractions and shorter words).

A *third* mistake many writers make is to forget to ask for a gift in a specific amount for a specific purpose by a specific date. For example, many letters are missing something like the following: "Please send a gift of $100 in the next 10 days so that we'll be able to provide a summer camp scholarship for a deserving student."

A *fourth* and very sad shortcoming in many fundraising

letters is that they are unreadable because of the way they've been designed. The cause is a worthy one and the letter is well written, but it turns out that it will take too much work on the part of the reader to comprehend what you're saying.

Remember, even your best donors spend very little time glancing at your letters, and your best prospects are older persons — many of whom no longer have the visual acuity of that 25-year-old staff person who designs your fund raising mail. Indented paragraphs, a serif typeface, 12-point type size, and paragraphs no more than seven lines long — all of these are essential to readability.

In addition to being readable, a fundraising letter should also look like a letter. A *fifth* mistake I see is foregoing a salutation, even if it's only "Dear Friend." (And don't say "Dear Friends," because then it's no longer a personal letter to an individual donor.) And be sure to have a traditional closing and signature — "Sincerely, (signature), typed name, title." If you're able to personalize your letters, then be sure to include a date, an inside address, and a personal salutation ("Dear Mr. Murphy").

A *sixth* "sin" I've noticed in lots of letters is that, paradoxically, the letters are too short but the sentences and the words are too long. Remember, almost all of your donors aren't staff members and only a few of them are dedicated volunteers. You need to use some paper (preferably recycled paper) to provide some background, give some examples, and explain why a contribution is needed now. However, the story you tell will be more comprehensible and persuasive if most of your sentences are 12 to 14 words long. And don't trip up your readers with too many big words.

The *seventh* sin is in many ways the most deadly — the lack of gratitude. Perhaps fundraisers feel they work so hard that they forget their donors are extraordinary individuals in their own right. If you're writing to your current donors, use the second or third paragraph to thank them for their past support. And be sure to express appreciation and gratitude again before you close the letter. If you're writing prospective donors, communicate respect and appreciation for their civic-mindedness, their leadership in the community, or their understanding of urgent issues.

P.S. Don't forget to include a P.S. in almost all of your fund-raising letters. Use the postscript to suggest a deadline, offer a premium, or add an extra reason to respond quickly to your appeal for funds.

44.

Misconceptions about Writing Letters

One of the most crippling misconceptions about letter writing is that it's hard and something to labor over. Not so. The secret of writing effective fundraising letters is to write quickly and naturally. To let the words *flow* from your fingers, to *talk* a "blue streak" on paper.

We're wary of people who choose their words too carefully, and we seldom vote for political candidates who appear to be "thinking" while they're speaking. Donors write checks because they feel a personal and comfortable connection with your organization and that starts with your writing.

Of course, once you've spewed out your purple prose, you must go back and rewrite. And rewrite again. Too many drafts can turn your letter into a stiff and convoluted essay, but I worry if my letters haven't gone through *three* drafts.

In fact, one of the primary reasons I edit my letters is that, in my haste in putting words on paper, I sometimes slip into "fine literature." I want to make sure my letter does feel like conversation – that it does indeed break the rules of good grammar and conventional prose. In other words, you edit fundraising letters so they don't seem "written" at all.

As I edit letters written by myself and others, there are at least seven practices that fly in the face of what many believe is good grammar or fine writing:

1) Contractions – the bread and butter of conversational prose. In the minds of many executive directors, the use of contractions is probably the single most offensive aspect of direct mail writing. But even the most educated and elegant leader can't avoid using this shorthand when speaking.

2) Frequent use of "I" – the singular voice that our school teachers tried to drum out of our essays, in an effort to achieve "objectivity."

3) Beginning sentences with "and" – one of my favorite connectors that encourages readers to keep reading (actually "listening" because that's the way we talk with friends).

4) Liberal use of dashes – they're so handy for linking phrases together in an "illogical" manner that helps the reader jump from one thought to another. They also serve as visual "breaks" that evoke the "breaths" we take when we're talking enthusiastically with our friends.

5) Short paragraphs without worrying about whether the sentences belong together – often just one or two sentences and never more than seven lines. Fundraising letters are read very quickly and with only partial attention, so you must make them easy to read.

6) Incomplete sentences – without a subject and predicate, missing either or both a noun and a verb. Even just one word. Really. We don't *talk* in complete sentences. If your computer

screen doesn't have a bunch of squiggly green lines (Microsoft WORD's grammar warning), then you haven't written a fundraising letter.

7) Redundancy and repetition – using the same words over and over as well as repeating arguments made earlier. In school, we were encouraged to rephrase. We were taught to organize our points in a logical progression from thesis to conclusion. But we know readers of fundraising letters don't read in a sequential pattern, so we can't ever leave them wondering about referents. And we can't rely on having our strongest argument appear only once in a letter. In a sense, almost every sentence – and surely every paragraph – has to stand on its own.

Please don't conclude that I believe in sloppy writing. Woe to you if you throw good grammar out the window. And you can't simply transcribe your oral speech onto paper. In reality, your syntax should be simpler, and you must avoid the trite phrases and other "empty words" that populate our speech. Your fundraising appeal will fall short if it sounds like an essay or an editorial, but ultimately your letter – filled with conversational prose – is still a letter to be read.

45.

Crafting Letters that Respect Your Donors

The best way to interest your readers in your letters is to focus on them. Begin by thanking your donors for their contributions. If the giving has been recent enough and generous enough, refer to the month the individual gave his or her gift: "Your gift in March of this year was a really big boost for our work on behalf...."

This approach also makes sense when "dunning" may seem most appropriate – that is, when you're writing to donors or members (especially members) whose giving has lapsed. You'll find that most people who have stopped giving to your organization don't realize how long ago it was that they sent a gift.

The language I like best for informing lapsed and inactive contributors is as follows: "According to our records, your last gift was in April of 2000. If you've sent a contribution that we've overlooked, please let us know. But I do hope you'll stay with us and continue your support of ...."

Of course, writing letters like this presumes that you keep accurate and up-to-date giving histories. Indeed, recording the amounts and the dates of an individual's gifts – and having easy access to this information – are *the* most important requirements of any database program or outside service you use. Much more important than some of the bells and whistles touted by software companies.

Keep in mind that it's also easier to show your respect and gratitude – and avoid "dunning" your donors – if you plan a mailing schedule with at least a half dozen different types of letters. Perhaps a long, newsy letter at the beginning of the year – one that lays out your organization's plans for the year. Another might be more visual – with lots of photographs and captions.

A third mailing might be a very brief note asking your donors to match their last gift. Or let them know you haven't heard from them for awhile. A fourth appeal might focus on a very specific project or tell a story about someone who has benefited from your organization.

At least one mailing a year should talk about renewal (with follow-up letters to those who don't respond). And a final, year-end appeal could stress gratitude and appreciation for the donor's generosity in the past year.

For your most generous and frequent contributors, you may also wish to send the ultimate non-dunning appeal: a letter with information and *no* request for money and *no* reply device. Just the latest developments related to your organization's mission or a report about a specific project or program.

Just as you vary the content of your appeals, you should also use different sizes and formats (as long as you don't go overboard and spend lots of money on glossy, hard-to read (and handle) inserts). At least a few times a year, your active donors should receive mailings that arrive in closed-face envelopes with an address that looks typed.

Some organizations are so concerned about dunning their

members that they seem terrified of asking too often for contributions. But when you think of your donors as generous and exceptional individuals who care deeply about your work, then you have the *obligation* to communicate with them on a regular basis. And these special friends will be disappointed if you don't give them a variety of opportunities – throughout the year – to support that work with their gifts.

46.

Writing Checklist

Most organizations spend too much time worrying about the content of their fundraising letters. So they don't have time left to make sure they're communicating often enough with their donors or members. So I'll want to keep this writing checklist short.

1) If you're writing to your current donors or members, does your letter - within the first few paragraphs - thank the person for her generosity in the past and her loyal support? If you're writing to prospective donors, do you convey respect for their intelligence and interest or for their compassion and commitment?

2) Does your letter have a consistent emotional tone? Does the reader know you are angry or upset? That you're facing an urgent, life-threatening situation? Both of these emotions are effective in fundraising letters, but use them with care and selectivity. In most instances, you'll want your letters to have a warm and friendly feel.

3) Is your letter personal communication between the person who signs the letter and the recipient? Are there enough "you's" and "I's" - and have you used contractions and other informal words? Avoid the tendency to turn your fund raising letter into a

magazine essay or newsletter article.

4) Have you asked for a gift? Have you asked for a specific amount - or at least communicated how much you need to raise? Have you explained what the donor's gift will accomplish? And why you need the gift to be sent as soon as possible?

5) Two small points, but they have a big impact on the readability of your letters (and remember your readers quickly scan letters):

• Avoid long-run and complex sentences and

• Make sure the reader knows whom you are talking about when you use third person pronouns (he, she, and they). Your readers just won't take time to go back and figure out what you're talking about.

6) Does your letter have a P.S. that provides an additional persuasive reason to send a gift - or why it's urgent to send the gift now? "P.S. Your gift is tax-deductible" doesn't qualify as an effective P.S.

7) Finally, did you take the time to read your letter aloud one last time? Reading aloud - if possible, reading your letter to a co-worker or friend - will help you "trip over" the awkward phrases, the flimsy arguments, words that can't be pronounced, and sentences that can't be read in one breath. Then you'll have a chance to remove those "stumbling blocks" and make your fundraising appeal more effective.

47.

Distinctive Style of Fundraising Prose

The style used in fund raising letters serves the primary purpose of those letters - to move the reader to take out her checkbook and send off a gift today.

Easier said than done, though.

In fact, as I review dozens and dozens of letters prepared by nonprofit organizations, the biggest single flaw I see is that donors are being sent essays (or manifestos in some cases) rather than letters.

How is the style of an effective fundraising letter different from that of a good essay?

First, the letter needs to be friendly. That doesn't mean consistently cheerful, but it needs to feel like communication between two people who know each other, who care about each other, who count on each other for support and counsel.

That leads to the second characteristic - the style is informal, conversational, relaxed. That's why you'll see lots of contractions in good fund raising letters. Split verbs come up more often because that's the way we talk to each other (like "come up" rather than "occur").

Fundraising letters have this relaxed, informal style. But at the same time the prose is action-oriented. Often essays encourage reflection and, in some cases, assent. Letters to your donors, however, seek action - you want your readers to do something.

Short sentences ... active verbs ... compound sentence structure (rather than complex) ... and the frequent use of connectors ("and, so, in other words, that's why") all keep the reader moving through your letter and in an active frame of mind.

In part because of your prose style, recipients of your fundraising letter are reading very quickly. Of course, the biggest reason they give your letters so little attention is that your donors are busy. And even those with spare time are probably just glancing at your letter (it is, after all, just the mail!).

So another characteristic of fundraising writing is repetition and redundancy. Most readers look at the P.S. and the opening sentence and then skip around back and forth throughout the letter. Effective writers therefore repeat their key idea several places (and underline key words) in the letter and - most important - ask for the gift at least three times.

And because readers scan your letters, you need to be very careful about the use of pronouns. Your reader won't take time to figure out who or what you're referring to when you start a new paragraph with "it, he, or they." In a real sense, almost all of the words in each paragraph have to stand on their own - you can't count on the reader having read the previous paragraphs.

Finally, even though you're consciously using all these techniques, your letter must be respectful. Essays can sometimes effectively take a condescending or sarcastic posture. But fundraising letters need to start with gratitude - it's truly inspiring that the people you write are generous and conscientious enough to take their time and money to support your cause. Even when you're sending letters to prospective donors, you're writing to people who have had the good grace to support other organizations.

48.

How We Read Letters

From my experience, there is a process to opening a direct mail package. And it goes something like this.

Typically the person first glances at the name and address to make sure the letter is hers. Thus one of the most important steps in making a favorable impression is to strive for accurate and complete data entry of your donor's name and address.

If you use a closed-face envelope and if the address looks as though it were typed, then the recipient is much more likely to open your envelope. Of course, a handwritten address would be even better. But if you can't afford that hand addressed or typed look, then a window envelope beats an envelope with a label slapped on it.

Further, almost every test conducted by our firm shows that having *metered* postage – whether first class or nonprofit – gets a higher response. And, especially if you're mailing to your own members or donors, be sure to put your logo in the upper left-hand corner. My preference in most cases is to have the name of the person (and her title, if appropriate) in black typewriter font above or below the logo.

Now, once the recipient has pulled the letter out of the envelope, she will see if it has been "personalized" with her name and address and with a salutation. Of course, that's more expensive in most instances, so your letter typically needs to begin "Dear Friend" or "Dear Member" or some other greeting that isn't too wacky ("Dear Conservationist" is okay – "Dear Lover of All Things Green" is wacky). The impression given by these subtleties is that this is indeed a personal letter.

In most instances, the reader will then jump to the *end of the letter* to see who it's from. That's why we encourage organizations to print the signature in *blue* ink. This will stand out in contrast to the letter text, which can be any color you want as long as it's *black*. The signature should be somewhat legible (not a scrawl) and the signer's name and title should be printed below the signature.

The P.S. is the next item read. A good P.S. is able to summarize the main argument of the letter or provide a compelling reason for sending a gift today. In rare instances, a P.P.S. is warranted but only if the situation is truly urgent.

If your reader is still with you, she will then go back and read the first paragraph of your letter. The best lead paragraphs are one sentence long and include as least one "you." You may find it trite but if you're stuck, you can do a lot worse than "I'm writing to you today because...."

After that, what happens is anyone's guess because research shows that when people read their mail – often at the end of the day, standing up over the waste basket or recycling bin – their eyes wander all over the place. They tend to glance quickly at indented paragraphs or underlined phrases (if they're not too long). We haven't found that blue underlining or simulated handwritten notes in the margin increase response.

Whatever happens, it all takes place very quickly – usually

about 30 seconds. Even your best donors and most faithful members are scanning your letters. That's why indented paragraphs, a readable type face, simple sentence structure, and short paragraphs are essential no matter how educated your membership or donor base.

In fact, my most reliable research source – my wife Jan who gives to lots of organizations – doesn't even read the letters from her favorite groups until she's looked at the reply device. She'll often read out loud exactly what they want a gift for, and then check to see whether – in her opinion – the dollar amount requested is reasonable. She doesn't like reply devices where she has to fill in her name and address.

After she's decided whether to send a gift, then she will *go back* and read some of the letter – or all of it if she finds an interesting story or surprising facts. The letter, then, becomes important in making the case for the most generous gift possible and for sending that gift as soon as possible. The longer the donor or member holds onto that reply device, the less likely she is to send a gift.

Finally, in observing my wife for over 30 years and talking with hundreds of donors, I've never heard anyone say they gave to an organization because they were favorably impressed by the brochure that was enclosed. So perhaps the most important element of your mailing is what you leave out.

49.

Emotional Appeals

To understand the significance of emotions in fundraising letters, we need to remember the purpose of a letter.

The fundraising letter must motivate a donor (or prospective donor) to set down the letter, get out her checkbook, and mail you back a check *the same day* she receives your appeal. Emotional writing — when done well — creates a sense of movement and urgency.

In mailing after mailing we analyze, I see that 40 to 60 percent of all income is received in the first 10 days of response. If your readers aren't responding immediately, then the chances of success for your mailing are very slim. That's why we call it direct mail because we strive to have readers respond directly.

It's also called direct mail *fundraising* because our letters are directed to donors or prospective donors. You'll never succeed in direct mail fundraising — or be happy in your career — if you worry about those people (including your executive director and board members) who say, "I don't read all that direct mail because it's too emotional." Our job is to write to those who appreciate hearing from organizations they care about and who enjoy writing checks and mailing them back to you.

Those readers to whom you direct your appeals are likely to be women and men with deeply held values and beliefs. They often have a strong sense of justice and compassion. While they may be angry and upset about some things in life, they feel content, secure, and grateful. Most have raised families, have established themselves in their careers, or retired from full-time work.

They have time to reflect and discretionary income to contribute to efforts that express their values and beliefs. Touching stories and emotional appeals are the tools you use as a writer to help your donors experience the connection between your organization's programs and the values and beliefs you and your donors have in common.

It's this emotional connection that creates the bond of trust that allows your donors to feel comfortable committing what is, at one level, an irrational or unnatural act — giving money away.

Indeed, many Americans (especially attorneys and younger adults who know everything about life) would think it downright crazy to believe that sending off a $25 check ... in the mail, to strangers ... could do anything to make our world a better place.

Thank goodness there are millions of Americans who are sentimental enough to keep mailing off those contributions. We and they are better off for it.

As I look at the fundraising programs my firm serves, those that are most successful *balance* emotional appeals with more factual and abstract appeals. In fact, we know that in every donor base, there are those donors or members who prefer to send gifts in response to newsletters (that's why most newsletters should have reply envelopes bound in).

An effective direct mail program can't sustain itself on a steady diet of full-bore, high-charged crisis appeals. Your mailings should sometimes be very brief and straightforward. For example, we see great response from mailings that are simply notes stating, "It's been some time since we heard from you. According to our records, your last gift of $50 was in November 2001. Please continue to support our vital work by sending a gift today."

A balanced fundraising program will also include at least three or four letters a year that don't ask for money. Letters that provide information and progress reports, that serve to express appreciation for the donor's support and interest.

It's this mix of emotions and reason that will help your organization build long-term relationships with "sentimental" individuals who will be your most loyal donors.

50.

Emotions that Motivate

In the field of marketing, fear is recognized as one of the most potent motivators, particularly fear of loss. And some organizations (such as those fighting cancer or heart disease) use fear effectively. But there are other potent motivators to be aware of.

Anger is a frequently used motivator in direct mail fundraising. Anger over injustice, corruption, or discrimination.

That's why many appeals include reply devices that are petitions, or post cards that one sends off to elected officials or corporate big wigs. Anger works because it is an emotion that, by its nature, wants to express itself. When we're angry we want to do something, to take some action.

But, in my experience, most direct mail programs can't sustain themselves on fear or anger alone. For most of us, these are temporary emotions, and they seldom motivate us long enough and strongly enough to go to the trouble of leaving a charitable bequest to a nonprofit organization. And the ultimate purpose of direct mail fundraising isn't getting high response rates to appeals but rather acquiring and retaining donors who will stay with your organization over the long haul.

What, then, are some other motivators?

One of the most powerful is the desire to be appreciated. I haven't run across too many people who feel they hear too many "thank you's" in their daily lives. In focus group after focus group and in hundreds of individual conversations, I hear how much donors appreciate the thank you letters they receive from organizations (which helps to explain why some of the most successful mailings are those that begin by noting the donor's recent gift and thanking her again for her generosity).

Another powerful motivator is the opportunity to leave a legacy, to pass on to another generation values and beliefs and culture. Those who respond to direct mail appeals are, in most cases, in their 60s and 70s. They want to leave something to their children and grandchildren, something greater than material possessions. Earmarking their resources to ensure the work of a nonprofit organization can create a truly extraordinary legacy.

Here are a few additional motivations at work in direct mail fundraising:

1) The desire to participate, to be part of a larger movement: "When you join with others who share your conviction, you..."

2) Community or neighborhood pride: "When you support the Library Foundation, you help make this a stronger community."

3) A sense of history, of preserving the past: "Your gift will make sure this piece of our city's history is preserved as a lasting monument."

4) A hunger for information: that's why organizations with newsletters almost always have higher renewal rates and higher average gifts.

5) Compassion for those less fortunate, a determination to stop the suffering: "Your gift will literally save the lives of children in war-torn areas."

6) The drive to have an impact, to see something accomplished: "By making a gift now, you will make it possible to...."

7) To stay connected: "Please renew your membership and continue to be part of ...."

Successful direct mail programs make sure that, throughout the year, donors or members receive mailings that use different motivators. Just like good friends, nonprofit organizations relate to donors on many emotional levels.

51.

The Look of Personal Correspondence

Everyone who receives direct mail appeals knows that thousands of people are receiving the identical letter, that what they're holding isn't a piece of personal correspondence. And yet I'm constantly urging you to make your letter look personal. Why?

The rationale is custom and convention, which provide the foundation and framework for effective fundraising. That's exactly why you should strive to make your direct mail letters as personal as possible.

That means a salutation, indented paragraphs, liberal use of "I" and "you," a closing ("Sincerely" or "Yours truly" or "Warm regards"), and a readable signature (blue ink is best). And, yes, most fund raising letters will be more effective if you use the Courier (but not New Courier) typeface or Times Roman.

In other words, your letter should look like a letter – not like an essay or a brochure. The advantage of using a customary and conventional letter format is that your reader can focus on your message – and not be distracted or irritated (consciously or subconsciously) by the unconventional style you're using.

This personal style works because it is "old fashioned" – it evokes a style of communication that's familiar to your readers, the overwhelming majority of whom are over 50, many of whom are in their 70s. The biggest challenge in direct mail is that most nonprofit staff are in their 20s and 30s; they have trouble empathizing with the culture and values of those older adults who provide the philanthropic support of their organizations.

Another reason to use a personal style is that it is friendly and chatty. It helps bridge the distance between writer and reader. If I'm going to send you a check, I need to feel some bond with you. Not many people read an essay with long paragraphs, printed in san serif typeface, and then feel motivated to send a check to the author of that essay.

Indeed, it is the personal style of communication that enables the writer of a direct mail letter to ask in an explicit, direct way for the reader to send a gift. And, in the same style, it is natural to use language that *urges* and *encourages* and even *pleads* with the reader to make that gift.

The purpose of a direct mail letter is for the reader to *take action* – to respond directly (today!), to take out her checkbook, and write a check to your organization. The personal letter style is the most effective way to get that action because it can credibly use brief sentences, short words, and action verbs – all of which give a breathless quality to direct mail prose.

Finally, the personal style in direct mail works because it is *not* a ruse, but reflects reality – even though many who write these letters or who work in nonprofit groups don't realize it's true. Those who read *and respond* to your letters really do feel a *personal connection* to your organization. They feel – if only in an unconscious act of suspended disbelief – that you are their "friend" and that you are signing the letter "sincerely."

The intimacy of your letters isn't misplaced because, once a gift is made, you and the reader now share the most intimate connection in our society – the exchange of money (most people are much more comfortable talking about sex than about money). That's what philanthropy is all about – it's about friendship that uses one friend's money to achieve a greater good.

And it is exactly this intimate, personal style – this philanthropic conversation between friends – that makes very frequent use of the two words that sustain any effective direct mail program: "thank you."

52.

Words or Pictures?

I'll repeat what I said at the beginning of this section: the great paradox of direct mail fundraising is that hardly anyone "reads" the letters sent out with appeals, but a fundraising appeal without a letter hardly ever works. Let's be clear, *never* works. The exceptions are too few to worry about.

And it's dangerous, in most cases, to use a lot of photographs in your fundraising appeals.

The way you reach people's hearts in direct mail is not with photographs but with words. With stories that disturb or inspire. With language that soars, or is so chatty and friendly you can't help but feel comfortable.

To be sure, using words to touch hearts is difficult; our prose is often inadequate and incomplete. Nevertheless, letters, especially multi-page letters presented in old-fashioned typewriter face, work very well in fundraising. The question is why.

First, letters are what people are used to receiving. At one level, charitable giving is a habit of convention, and we break these conventions at our peril.

Even if the recipient doesn't read one word of your letter, she'll wonder why your package doesn't include one because that's what she's used to receiving. And if your package is too unusual, too full of visual images, then the recipient will feel uncomfortable, if only at a subconscious level. That discomfort will undercut the trust your readers need to feel if they're to take out their checkbooks and send you a gift.

Second, letters are personal. In survey after survey, people indicate that they make charitable contributions because they're asked to do so. Letters are the best way to say, "I'm writing to *you* to ask for *your* help. *Your* special gift will …." Photographs are by their nature impersonal; they don't speak directly to me as an individual even though I may find them appealing or attractive.

Third, letters are an ideal way to stimulate action. The purpose of direct mail fundraising is to get your readers to send a gift. Words, phrases, and sentences can all give instruction and direction to your reader. "P.S. Please take a moment right now to send off your membership gift." And the longer your letter the more often you can repeat and rephrase those admonitions to your reader.

Granted, photographs do have a role to play in direct mail. Some effective letters even have photographs spread throughout. Others will include one or more snapshots or a post card with a photographic image. And photographs are perfect for a newsletter or an informational mailing to your donors or even as an insert to accompany your thank you letter. Further, a photo – especially one with just two or three people with captivating eyes – can sometimes help your reply device stand out from the other elements of your mailing.

But, as useful as they are, photographs aren't essential and, in some of the tests we've conducted, they haven't led to increased response rates – only increased costs.

53.

Varying Your Thank You Letters

If you've been in fundraising for very long, you may struggle with how to vary your thank you letters, especially to those donors who give every year or several times throughout the year. Actually, you don't need to worry too much.

For donors, including multi-year donors, who make smaller gifts – say under $100 – quickly sending out brief pre-printed thank yous with simply the amount and date of the gift noted can be more effective than long-winded thank you letters that go out late.

It's also very effective to send out hand-written notes – they don't have to be long and they really stand out in the mail. Even if you're sending out word-processed letters or receipt-style thank yous, you can give them a fresh look by hand addressing the outer envelope. And be sure to change from time to time the size of your stationery, the paper stock, and ink colors you use in your thank you mailings.

Whether you write long or short thank you letters, here are six suggestions for opening lines:

1) Thank you! You send a gift year after year, and your faithful support is so very encouraging to the staff and volunteers. Your recent gift of $__ is especially helpful.

2) Your generous contribution of $__ arrived in today's mail. Thank you! Please know that your gift will be put to immediate use.

3) I'm writing on behalf of all the staff and volunteers here at XYZ organization. We are deeply grateful for your repeated gifts.

4) Thank you for your recent gift of $__. Your generosity demonstrates a genuine commitment to …(the cause or issue your organization addresses).

5) I'm writing to thank you for your gift of $__, which we received on December 14, 2003, and to report to you about a recent breakthrough we achieved – in part because of your generous support.

6) We really appreciate your gift of $__. It's so helpful to be able to count on friends like you who respond again and again to the work we do.

Another great way to keep from getting in a "thank you rut" is to call a couple of donors each day to thank them for their gifts. They will be pleasantly surprised to hear from you and they'll have a deeper sense that their gifts were appreciated. In addition, you'll also find out *why* these remarkable folks are sending you checks. You'll end up with several new ideas for new and creative thank you letters.

54.

Can Writing Be Learned?

Good direct mail writing can be learned. And re-learned. More importantly, writing for fundraising is almost never a "talent." It requires the constant and repeated use of "formulas" and a "return to the basics."

Certainly those to whom writing comes naturally have a leg up in this. But even the best writer can lose that all-important focus on the reader.

Perhaps most important is the ability to sound as though you're *talking* with just *one* reader. Further, direct mail appeals are effective when they *ask for a gift* – not just tell a well-written story. In fact, some people may be so overcome with the story that they don't get around to sending a gift. Again, finding that balance between presentation and solicitation requires real training and careful editing.

Attending workshops or reading books about writing increases the chance you'll learn a powerful secret: good direct mail letters are written very quickly – the roughest possible first draft – and then rewritten and rewritten. Not to take the life away from them

– or to satisfy some committee — but to remove those extra words and phrases that even the best writer inadvertently adds.

With fewer words and simpler sentences, a good writer adds clarity and quickens the pace for the reader. As an added benefit, the writing will sound more like friendly conversation – which is why direct mail writers read their letters aloud before they send them off to be printed.

Finally, there are some organizations where the letter is about an *idea* or a concept – rather than about people and their stories. Granted, it may be effective to represent that idea with a story. But that's not always possible or even advisable. And when you don't have the structure of character and plot that a story provides, you need even greater skill in writing.

Developing that skill involves learning from others – whether in a workshop, through reading about letter-writing techniques or by having your letters edited by others.

V.

KEY COMPONENTS OF YOUR APPEAL

It takes more than a strong letter to raise money through the mail. In the words of Mal Warwick, your objective should be to write a *package*, not a letter.

The letter is essential, of course, but it does its work best when your mailing includes other key elements that are discussed in this section.

The challenge is not only to include these key components in your appeals, but also to have those package elements interact in a way that reinforces your central message. Ultimately, that message should be "Please send your gift today."

Of course you'll want to balance the cost of each component against the probable return. As you perform that balancing act, remember our discussion about targeting your mailings in Part Three. The key to success in direct mail fundraising is to spend extra money on mailings that go to your most generous and responsive donors – and to use less expensive components for prospective donors or for those who have made smaller contributions.

As you put these components together into one package, you'll be making lots of decisions about paper and postage and inserts and the size of your mailing piece -- all with the ultimate aim of creating a look and tone that reinforces the written text of your appeal.

The pages that follow will guide you in that decision-making process – to help you avoid unnecessary expenses and create a mailing package that raises more money for your organization.

55.

Creating a Direct Mail Package

In more than 30 years of writing and sending out fundraising appeals, I've learned a lot of "rules" and even promulgated several myself. But for purposes here, let me distill my experience into six suggestions you might find helpful:

The first and most important dimension of direct mail fundraising is that it exists as a part of a larger, strategic plan for your organization's resource development. So every time you create a direct mail package ask yourself, "How does this fit in with everything else we're doing to secure our organization's future?"

Second, start with your donors. Try to be very clear who you're sending this package to. Study some donor records ... read some correspondence ... call up a couple of your members. What are their concerns? What do they like about your organization? What motivates them to contribute? And what specifically do you want them to do (often we forget the purpose of a fund raising letter is to encourage donors to take out their checkbooks and send you a generous gift today).

Third, don't write a letter. Write an entire package. Try to conceive of the outer envelope, letter, reply device, and reply envelope as one unified, interconnected communication vehicle to your donor. Sometimes, it helps me to sketch out a package — or to create a "dummy" with actual envelopes, letter, and reply device. One of the bonuses of this step is that you'll make sure your letter or reply device fits inside the envelope!

Fourth, work quickly. Write fast. Don't stop midstream. Your style will be much more natural and your logic more coherent if you create your package all in one sitting. You'll be more passionate and creative as well, because you're less likely to censor yourself when you write quickly. Of course, you'll need to set aside time to re-read and rework your first rough draft.

Fifth, read your letter (and other elements of your package) aloud. Don't skip this step! Reading aloud helps you make sure your package is natural, comfortable, friendly, and comprehensible. If you can't easily pronounce a word, it's the wrong word to use. If a sentence is too long to read in one breath, cut it into two or three sentences. And there's nothing like reading aloud to discover those embarrassing lapses in logic or sequencing. (In fact, I read aloud as I type out the first, rough draft of my letters.)

Sixth, don't let a "creative" graphic designer ruin your package. Avoid a trendy, arty look. Do everything you can to protect the readability of your package: white, cream or light gray papers ... courier type face for the letter ... indented paragraphs ... 12-point as the minimum point size for any "typeset elements" (except for "regulatory rhetoric" which can be in smaller type) ... and black ink for any lengthy text (including the letter). Yes, this will make your package look old-fashioned — and that will encourage donors to trust you enough to send a gift.

And here's my bonus suggestion: Be willing to break any of these "rules" if you believe you have a better way of building a lasting relationship with your donors.

56.

Checklist for Evaluating Your Finished Package

When you're looking over your mailing package one last time before sending it to the printer, don't hold on to it for too long. Get it into the mail.

Over the past two decades I've met and talked with hundreds of fundraisers. I've been struck that many are quite knowledgeable, yet they seem to accomplish very little in terms of results. My conclusion: when it comes to raising money, it's most important to just do it. Ask early and ask often, recognizing you'll make mistakes along the way. Don't let your knowledge or the "industry rules" paralyze you with analysis or anxiety. In fact, some of the best direct mail packages have been conceived quickly, almost recklessly.

Nonetheless, it is wise to take a few moments – before the presses get rolling – to review the package for both small mistakes and glaring errors. But even before you review the package, be sure to double-check the list you're mailing to. Remember, *who receives your package* affects response more than how attractive or compelling your mailing is.

When reviewing a package, read it aloud – from outer envelope, the letter, reply device, and reply envelope. If possible, have a second person also read it aloud. When you do this, you'll find words or phrases your tongue trips over. Get rid of these hard-to-pronounce words and straighten out that tortured syntax.

Reading aloud also reveals arguments or logic that are preposterous or nonsensical. And you'll discover whether the central concept – the unifying theme – is clearly presented in all elements of your mailing.

In addition to reading your package aloud, this is the time to ask yourself, "Will this letter and reply device motivate the reader to take out a checkbook and send a contribution?" The purpose of direct mail fundraising in not the reader's admiration or even assent with your arguments, but rather his or her direct response of sending you a check as early as possible.

Among the most common errors I see in direct mail packages are those involving the fit and completeness of the reply device. Does the reply device show through the window? Does it fit into the return envelope? Have you included your organization's name and address on the reply device? Are there suggested gift amounts (unless you're testing no set amount)?

The final check should be whether you're complying with postal regulations. For example, does the size and shape of your envelope avoid surcharges? You'll also want to weigh your package, particularly if some or all of it is being mailed first-class. It's very easy to exceed one ounce. The return of all your wonderful mailings by the post office for affixing additional postage is a shock you'll always want to avoid.

57.

The Five Key Variables

Didn't Yogi Berra say something about baseball being 90 percent mental and the other half perspiration? And Tom and Ray of National Public Radio's "Car Talk" frequently mention the "third half" of their one-hour radio show.

In other words, the elements of direct mail fundraising are *all* equally important *in their own way* and merit the greatest possible weight. But let me attempt to assign a weight to each.

At our firm, we tell organizations that the list is half (50 percent) of what makes direct mail work. I think we say that because we want them to feel good about paying us for all the other things we do (and these other tasks do take a lot of time). But an argument could be made that, in one sense, *the list is at least 80 percent* or as much as 90 percent of the equation.

One reason the list is so important is that direct mail fundraising is *not* about converting non-donors into donors. Rather, our mailings, especially those designed to acquire new members or new donors, seek out those who are *already* donors (but perhaps not yet donors to your organization) and, ideally, already interested in the issue or problem you address.

The list is also crucial because a relatively small percentage of all Americans exercise their philanthropy by sending checks in response to direct mail. This small (but truly powerful and generous) percentage is highly educated, is at least in their mid-forties and usually older, own their own homes, often attends church or synagogue, reads newspapers and magazines, listens to public radio, and has household incomes of $70,000 and above.

When it comes to your own donor or membership base, the list remains pivotal because about 10 to 15 percent of your donors will account for 80 to 85 percent of all your organization's contributed income. So you'll want to make sure (through the truly hard work of database segmentation) that your most responsive and generous donors receive more mailings. Their mailings should, in most cases, use more personalization, ask for larger gifts, and use first class postage on the outer reply envelopes.

Oops! You caught me sneaking over into the "offer" (the gift amount you ask for and how you ask for it), and package design.

If the list has 50 percent weight, then the *offer is about 25 percent*.

In direct mail fundraising, the offer is important because you don't want to ask — except under unusual circumstances — donors who've given you $100 to make a $25 contribution or a $2,500 gift. Indeed, one of the key challenges for most mature fund raising programs is to prevent $100 donors from sliding back down to $25. It takes four $25 gifts to make up for one $100 gift. So it's critical that you ask donors to maintain — and increase — the size of their gifts.

The offer is also important when you're recruiting new members or donors. The people on the lists you're mailing will resist making initial contributions of $100 or $500 (fortunately, a few delightful folks will). Thus, if you want to build a base of donors through direct mail acquisition, you need to be offering membership or support at $15, $25, or as high as $35.

Finally, the offer has weight because it's how you show the donor or potential donor the impact of her gift: "Your gift of $55 will bring clean water to an entire village in Africa." Or, "When you join with a gift of $35, you'll receive our monthly magazine as well as our special resource packet."

Obviously, this offer won't have any weight unless it's read (and taken seriously). That's why *package design is about 15 percent* (yes, we're up to 90 percent so far).

The envelope serves the purpose of getting recipients to open it so they can then read your compelling offer or request for a gift. Closed-face envelopes with what looks like a typed address or even a hand-written address, and with first class postage, get opened most often.

However, that's a very expensive way to mail, so this combination should be used primarily for the responsive, generous 15 percent of your donor base. For prospective donors and the less responsive segments of your membership that you mail bulk rate, you may want to test "teasers" (URGENT ... Please open immediately ... The favor of your reply is requested) and over-sized envelopes.

Once the reader is inside, the package design influences response because it can encourage the recipient to grab the checkbook, write the check, and enclose it with the reply device in the reply envelope. That happens when the package is readable (selecting the right typeface and laying it out on the page so it looks like a friendly, approachable letter) and when the reply device is easy to use.

The design or format of the package is also critical because, in more cases than not, including a brochure or other insert *decreases* response rates. In many cases, if the letter isn't two, three, or four pages, response rates go down as well.

To get a three- or four-page letter, you need some *copy or written text*. The words and sentences you use in your appeals have about *7 percent weight*. But, in another sense, if the list is 90 percent, the copy is the other half.

That's why smart organizations pay thousands of dollars to copywriters or freelance writers to create their direct mail appeals. The writing process is the way you achieve a coherent, persuasive interaction with donors or prospective donors. Good copy weaves together into a seamless whole the offer (gift request), the issues and concerns of your readers (the list), and the design of the package.

In that writing process, though, the specific words and phrases aren't all that important. In fact, one of the big tragedies of nonprofit fundraising is that most organizations waste so much time obsessing and arguing about whether the letter is complete, accurate, and precise enough that they fail to communicate often enough with their members or donors. And the search for the Holy Grail of the perfect letter often keeps organizations from sending letters that use short words, short sentences, and conversational syntax. What's important about copy is that it's easy to read, strikes a friendly tone, and expresses appreciation and admiration.

Finally, we come to *timing, which is just 3 percent* because it really doesn't matter that much when you send your appeals. You can't control events in the recipient's life (if they're on vacation, they're not going to open your letter) nor can you control how long the post office will take to deliver your mail if you send it bulk or standard rate.

Of course, if there's a major disaster or world-shaking event that's in the news and related to what your group does, then by all means use a package you can send out quickly. And, for heaven's sake, be sure to send out mailings at year-end and in January when donors and prospects are most responsive.

Timing does become 100 percent of the equation in the sense that your direct mail program will succeed only if you have a regular schedule of mailings — and if you stick to that schedule.

And you need to make sure your mailing schedule gives donors and prospects enough opportunities to support your organization. That enables your donors to time their gifts according to their interests and ability to give. And frequent mailings to your responsive and generous donors allows them to time additional gifts because they care so much about what you do.

To sum up then, if I were pressed, and if it's clearly understood that each of the factors is 100 percent important, I'd weigh them this way: list (50 percent), offer (25 percent), package and design (15 percent), copy (7 percent), timing (3 percent).

58.

Seeking Brand Recognition

While you should strive to give a similar look or unified design to your organization's mailings, you should at the same time make a continual effort to pique curiosity with different looking packages (the same style and format for every mailing will be deadly).

Why members and donors like packages to look familiar:

1) Even folks who are retired are very busy and receive lots of mail (in large part, because they're well educated and usually well off), so they don't have a lot of patience or time to figure out who's sending them a letter.

2) As much as you wish it weren't the case, your organization isn't the major focus of the donor's life - nor is it probably even the organization she cares most about. In other words, she isn't "bored" or "tired" of the way your mailings look because lots of other mail (and lots of living) has taken place since the last mailing you sent her.

3) Even though your organization isn't the center of the person's life, there was something about your mailing that did appeal to the donor. Likely, it was the name of your organization, perhaps even your logo, maybe a photograph, or a key phrase. Donors do like the organizations they support, so be careful about changing too dramatically your visual image.

Why you should vary the look of your mailings:

1) Your donors - especially your best donors - get lots of mail from lots of organizations, and they assume that duplicates abound. So you want to avoid having your donors make the snap judgment, "Oh that's the mailing I received last week."

2) Two of those most effective ways to boost your response are to spend more money to personalize mailings and to use first class postage on both the outer envelope and on the reply envelope. But these techniques are costly and it isn't cost-effective to use them in all your mailings. So plan on varying your use of personalization and postage from mailing to mailing.

3) Different-sized envelopes do convey - perhaps subliminally - different messages or tones. Most donors perceive smaller envelopes as more intimate while oversized envelopes convey substance. Often the nature of your letter strongly suggests using either a smaller or larger envelope.

4) When you have a crisis or an emergency, your direct mail package should "shout." Bright colors, bold type, special "urgent" outer envelopes are appropriate if your situation is truly critical. (You'll create a real backlash if your message isn't convincingly urgent, or if you use this format too frequently.)

5) Donors tell us (and renewal rates support their words) that they like newsletters and informational mailings. These will necessarily look different. You can even let some of the young people on your staff exercise their "creative flair" in designing these newsletters - as long as they use a serif typeface of at least 11 points.

59.

Techniques that Repel

I've been writing appeal letters for almost 30 years now, and to be honest I'm less certain than ever about what works and what doesn't work. About all I know for sure is that donors give despite everything we do to discourage them.

Direct mail fundraising works because we happen to get our letters (and return envelopes) into the hands of generous Americans who want to help make this a better world. Thank goodness for them!

As we try to earn the confidence of these generous donors, it is always appropriate – at the right time and in the right circumstance – to break one or more of the sacred rules of fund raising. But one of the great dangers in fund raising is taking too much time and spending too much energy trying to craft the perfect appeal. It's much more important to keep communicating with your donors.

Along the way, you're sure to make some mistakes and even turn off some donors. But those mistakes are a great opportunity to apologize to your donors – and so strengthen your relationship with them. (Anyone who has been doing this work for very long has received a check in response to an apology letter.) And, perhaps most important, missteps take you down the all-essential path of experience.

To help you learn from your mistakes more quickly, I can offer you a list of things to think twice about – perhaps three or four times – before you proceed:

1) Are you sending an essay rather than a letter? Fundraising is personal communication with lots of "I" and "you" – *not* your organization's manifesto to the world or profound reflection on reality.

2) Did you follow the designer's advice and use blue or green ink for the text of the letter? Black is the *only* ink color to use if you want more than just a few lines of text to be read. Signatures can be printed in dark blue, and that adds to your letter's verisimilitude.

3) Does your letter end with *two* signatures? Only *one* person can send a personal, friendly, and persuasive letter.

4) Have you included a glossy and intricate brochure along with your letter? Well, you've certainly raised the cost of your mailing – and lowered the possibility that the reader will respond. Donors want to read personal and friendly letters.

5) Is your reply device too large to fit into the reply envelope? An ideal reply device repeats how the gift will be used and includes the donor's name and address, suggested gift amounts (with an option for the donor to specify an amount), and your organization's name and address. Donors are willing to fold this reply device around a check – if that folding seems natural. But it's great if the donor's check and reply device fit snuggly in the

return envelope.

6) To save money and keep your board happy, did you make sure your letter fit onto a single page? Those who send you money care about your organization, and are likely to be well educated and to enjoy reading. Take as much space as you need to tell your story –– and to make sure your paragraphs are seven lines or shorter, your margins are adequate (white space to breathe), and your type is large enough to read.

7) Have you talked about the state of the economy and your organization's budget shortfall? Those two themes are likely to inspire your donors to hold on to their money. Direct mail appeals succeed when you talk about the opportunities your organization has to make a difference – and how the donors' support will make all this possible.

I'm sure there are many other "things to avoid" in direct mail, but I don't want you to spend too much time reading about fundraising. Instead, get out there and start making those mistakes!

60.

Obsolete Techniques

Today, as I write this, I know there are definitely techniques that are obsolete and should be avoided. But, if you ask me tomorrow, my list might be different. Which is to say that, even though they've become "obsolete," old, or over-worked, various techniques should be tested or tried from time to time. And, conversely, some of the package formats and well-turned phrases that are working so well today must be repeatedly tested – to make sure they haven't lost their effectiveness.

Right now, though, I tend to discourage people from using any of the following:

1) Nonprofit stamps on the outer envelope. They cost more and donors tell us the stamps broadcast "junk mail." Almost all the testing we've done suggests that postage *metered* at the nonprofit rate works as well – if not better – than nonprofit stamps.

2) First class stamps on the outer envelope. Using metered first-class postage is usually less expensive – especially because you can use pre-sort postage. And it may make readers feel "safer" in opening their mail because the mail seems "business-like." In the area just below the meter, you can print the words "FIRST CLASS"

so your recipient senses this is important mail.

3) Lift notes. Years ago, these extra letters – actually little, short notes – were very popular. Often a different person from the one who signed the letter would write a brief endorsement of the organization or provide an additional, urgent reason to send a gift. Our testing hasn't found very many instances where this extra letter has "lifted" response – and it has definitely increased costs.

4) Green or red signatures. Actually, this isn't an obsolete technique for me because I've never used it. And fortunately, I see fewer and fewer mailings that utilize this technique. But I'm designating this as an "obsolete technique" in the hope that it will disappear completely. It is crucial that your fundraising letters have a bold and legible signature – ideally in dark blue ink and with the person's name and title "typed" below the signature. If it can't be printed in blue, then use black ink – not some cute color.

5) Teasers on outer envelopes. There are some exceptions, but in almost every instance, the use of a question or catchy phrase (for example, "You can make a difference!") actually *lowers* response.

6) Blank outer envelopes – no return address. Even before the Anthrax scare, these envelopes had lost any illusion of mystery. Envelopes without any printing are quickly tossed into the recycling bin. People *want to know* who is sending them a letter.

That's why, in addition to the organization's name and address, we often include the name of the individual who signs the letter. Remember, those who contribute to nonprofit organizations like the work these organizations do – so your name is your best calling card. And, if your organization's name doesn't make it clear who you are, you should add a brief tagline to make it clear what you do.

7) Business Reply Envelopes. Again, a handful of organizations will get a higher response if they use all those bars of dark print and say "No Postage Necessary" and "Business Reply Mail" in big bold letters. But test after test – for organization after organization – shows that asking donors to use their own stamps gets the same or higher response. And you avoid the cost and the inconvenience of business reply mail.

8) Credit card option. Lots of organizations want to give their donors a chance to make a gift via their credit card. Again, our tests have shown that this option doesn't lead to more gifts and, in some cases, discourages response. There's also the additional cost of the credit card discount your organization must pay. To be sure, you may get larger gifts this way, but your organization should be using direct mail to get more gifts from the largest number of donors or prospects.

9) Reply devices with gift options that range from $1000 to $10. I'm not sure this ever worked, but it's certainly become "more obsolete." If you're appealing to your own donors or members, you should base the gift request on their giving history – giving them, at most, three options: their highest gift ever and two options higher than that. In some instances, you can suggest a big upgrade but the case for a truly significant gift better be strong.

As you acquire new donors, don't worry about the handful of folks who will give you $500 or $1000 gifts. Most new donors will make initial gifts in the $15 to $100 range. Test to see what the best initial gift level is – and then offer three or, at most, four options on your acquisition reply devices.

10) Black, muddy, and hard-to-read photos. In the good old days, direct mail packages could get away with this. And in the bad new days, the proliferation of inexpensive digital cameras

appears to have generated a plethora of fuzzy photos.

Printing technology makes crisp color photos almost identical in price to black and white photos. And because of advances in technology, recipients have higher expectations when it comes to photos. If you can't use good photos, get by without them.

Reviewing this list of obsolete techniques is a reminder that direct mail fundraising works best when the reader feels she is receiving a personal letter from someone who respects her generosity – and trusts her desire to support endeavors she truly cares about.

61.

The Role of Inserts

First let me say, in my experience, that the most effective insert for direct mail fund raising is the "buck slip" — typically a 3-1/2 by 8-1/2 inch sheet of yellow or canary stock, printed in black ink. As for when to use an insert, here are some instances when it might make sense:

One that comes to mind quickly is when there's some late-breaking news — an emergency or crisis situation — that adds to the urgency of your appeal. In one recent instance, a buck slip worked very well because the late-breaking news was about a challenge match for all membership gifts made within a specific month.

Another good reason to include an insert is when the leaders of the organization feel strongly that the letter should have more than one signature. The problem is that dual — or even worse, multiple — signatures undercut the sense of "I-you" communication that is the foundation of effective direct mail. Thus I often suggest that one person sign one letter, and that a second letter — usually 7 inches by 10 inches on a different colored stock — be signed by a second person.

A third case in which an insert can be effective is when your package includes a "front-end premium." Mailing labels, stamps, a beautiful color postcard, or a bookmark are some of the commonly offered items. Of course you need to test whether these inserts actually increase response for your particular organization.

A final rationale for inserts is one that has become increasingly important with the new accounting standards which mandate a "call to action" is when you wish to allocate some of your direct mail expenses to public education. A postcard to be signed and mailed by the recipient to an elected official or a corporate mogul can be effective for both fundraising and public relations.

As you consider these possible inserts, be sure to evaluate them against the central premise or concept that guides each package or fundraising appeal. For example, if your letter is about the financial crisis faced by your organization, then including a beautiful full color postcard belies your message.

Also consider whether your insert might work more effectively as part of the reply device. Often, we will have a tear-off portion of the reply device that includes a map, photo, a fact sheet, or even short additional message.

Finally, I hope all these suggestions about inserts reinforce the original premise behind these questions: namely, inserts *don't work* in most situations. Inserts seem to distract your prospects and donors from reading the letter and from using the reply device to send their gift.

In nearly three decades of direct mail fundraising, I've only seen a handful of cases where a brochure or a "lift letter" have increased response rates. So, when it doubt, leave it out.

62.

Multiple Signatures

In large part, fund raising letters work because they simulate and evoke a personal letter - correspondence from one person to that other person's good friend: "I'm writing you today because you and I...." Multiple signatures turn letters into essays and destroy any sense of one-to-one communication.

This breakdown of the "I-you" connection is especially evident when it comes to the two essential qualities of an effective fundraising letter:

A) Saying thank you to the donor for his or her previous support, and

B) Asking for a specific gift.

Having more than one signature takes all the sincerity out of a thank you - no two individuals can express something so personal as appreciation in the same way. And one of the reasons we do things - like send charitable contributions - is because someone asks us. That request is much more powerful when we perceive it as a personal request, when we believe someone (not a group or a committee) is counting on us to come through.

I suspect, too, that if an organization had a planned schedule of mailings, then they'd be less likely to use letters with multiple signatures. Why? Because some organizations consciously or unconsciously feel their appeal lacks credibility or urgency. For them, adding one or more extra signatures solves that dilemma.

However, a better solution is a series of mailings throughout the year, signed perhaps by different individuals with a strong connection to the organization. A planned, scheduled fund raising program - not a letter with multiple signatures - is the most effective way to build a credible and urgent case for support.

If you're sending out six or more appeals to your donors, then different persons can sign different letters. The executive director, chair of the board, the program director, and your favorite aunt can all get their chance.

Then too, letters with multiple signatures sometimes reflect internal conflicts between the executive director and the board, or between the development staff and the chief executive. The hope is that all those signatures will somehow create some political detente or power sharing.

Rather than adding signatures to your letter, why not try some proven direct response techniques?

For example, you can add a brief note to your fund raising package to reinforce the main message or suggest an additional urgent reason for sending a gift. The board chair, or someone famous with a credible connection to your cause or organization, or a recipient of your organization's services are all good candidates for signing this note.

In other instances, a follow-up letter sent two or three weeks after the first appeal can be signed by a different individual from the first letter. And, in very rare instances, you may want to include a statement of principles or an endorsement signed by a number of individuals.

But, in all these cases, the primary letter should be a highly personal one signed by just one individual.

63.

URGENT! Telegrams

In my experience, pseudo-telegrams with an 'URGENT' outer envelope work consistently. The response rate is almost always above average, though the average gift is typically lower.

Even if you don't like the "fake" look of these urgent appeals, and even if your organization rarely has an emergency or crisis, it's worth your while to think about why they work and apply the lessons to *all* of your fund raising letters.

1) At least half of all those who respond to your fund raising letters do so within days of receiving them. *Immediate response* determines success in direct mail, and the urgent format underlines the need for quick action.

2) Most organizations write their urgent appeals quickly and don't spend a lot of time editing them. Direct mail letters aren't like good wine — aging helps them very little. A drawn-out writing process and repeated editing suck the life out of far too many fund raising letters.

3) For some reason, the urgent format seems to give organizations and writers a sense of "permission" to be *bolder and more direct in asking for a response*. All too often, regular fundraising

letters go on and on about organizational concerns and beat around the bush when it comes to asking for a gift.

4) The most effective urgent formats are simple, straightforward, and economical. That means net income is higher. Their pre-printed, standardized elements make them just about the cheapest way to send a personalized appeal to your donors, even if you have a relatively small mailing list.

If you decide to try a telegram or urgent format, here are some guidelines to consider:

A) Your piece doesn't have to look like a telegram and the text needn't be in all upper case.

B) Shop around for the best vendor. Prices vary greatly, depending on what you're looking for.

C) Don't manufacture an emergency or crisis. Integrity and honesty foster the greatest long-term return from your donors.

D) You simply must not use an urgent format more than once or twice a year. Otherwise, you erode your credibility with your donors, evidenced by a decline in gift amounts.

E) Be sure to write a *special thank-you letter* in response to gifts made to meet your crisis or emergency. And, in your newsletter, report on the results of the actions your group took to meet the urgent challenge.

64.

Self-Mailers

Why does all direct mail look alike? Because that's what works.

A conventional package — containing an outer envelope, letter, reply device, and return envelope — is almost always the horse to bet on in direct mail fundraising.

Why don't more organizations use self-mailers (those self-connected pieces that contain a letter, reply device, and reply envelope)? Because they don't work. So even though they're less expensive, they don't really save you any money because the response rates and average gifts are almost always lower. I'm sure there are exceptions, and if you're sending out lots of mailings and have room in your budget, then you may want to test self-mailers.

Do we know why donors prefer the "classic" or conventional package?

Much of what we say about the appearance of direct mail packages is an effort to explain — after the fact — the results of testing. In other words, we're not really certain *why* donors prefer one kind of mailing over another; we just see that the results are better when we stick to the conventional package.

But I can offer some explanation, as I watch my family members open and respond to direct mail appeals, and there have been several studies of what people do with direct mail (eye-motion studies and observation behind one-way mirrors).

Recipients of direct mail seem to like all the separate, disparate pieces that make up a package. They enjoy writing the check, tearing it out, putting the check and the reply device in the envelope. Others save the reply device and reply envelope and put it with their bills to pay.

And almost all direct mail donors at least glance at the letter. That's probably why having a separate, stand-alone letter is so effective. And why we work so hard to make it *look like a letter* — Courier or Times Roman typeface, indented paragraphs, salutation, closing (with a signature), and, of course, the P.S.

One final advantage of these traditional packages with separate elements is that they can almost always be printed and mailed more quickly than specialized one-piece self-mailers (which require elaborate pre-press set-up). That means it's easier for you to make sure your donors are contributing to your current and urgent needs.

65.

Colored Envelopes

It's definitely worth testing the use of color stock for envelopes. In larger acquisition mailings, you always need to see if there's some factor that can lift response. And, in large quantities, colored envelopes can be used without raising costs too much. Some vendors can even print a "color wash" on standard white envelopes.

Further, when you're sending a number of appeals throughout the year to your faithful members and donors, there's value in varying the color (and size) of the envelopes you use. Otherwise, your donors might think that they've already received the mailing – or that it's just more of the same.

But be careful on at least a couple of counts: First, the postal service has standards about the contrast between the ink used to address an envelope and the envelope background. So dark colors can get your mailing rejected at the post office. Second, in small and medium quantities, special envelope stock or sizes can be *very* expensive. It would take a huge lift in response to offset the increased cost.

If you want to stand out, sometime it's actually cheaper to use a standard closed-face envelope with a laser or inkjet addressing process that looks like a typewritten address.

66.

Cardinal Rules of Carrier Envelope Copy

When in doubt, leave the teaser out! At the very least, test that clever question or hard-hitting statement that you see blazoned across many outer or carrier envelopes. In many cases, a teaser can depress response – perhaps because it screams "junk mail" or because what you thought was clever merely confuses your reader.

It is still the case, though, that teasers can lift response – especially if they relate to current events or pressing matters. Here at our firm we've also found that "teasers" related to membership renewal or membership re-activation boost response.

In general, though, my preferred carrier envelope has the organization's name and address – along with the logo – in the upper left corner. This is sometimes called the "corner card." A dark blue, green, or brick-red are all strong colors to use. I like having the name of the signer of the letter – along with his or her title – printed in black ink (using the same type font as the letter text) above or below the corner card. Finally, I'm a big fan of metered postage – whether it's first class or nonprofit.

While this is my *preferred* carrier or outer envelope, it's still not my *most favorite*. What I really like – and what really works – is a plain, closed faced envelope with a handwritten address. Needless to say, it costs a lot of money to use this envelope, but it can be amazingly effective with your very best donors or with those who are lapsed in their support.

And, of course, it's the ideal format for *you* to use – when you send handwritten thank-you notes in response to those generous gifts from those individuals who care so much about your organization.

67.

Peel-Off Stickers

From time to time, you've probably received a mailing from a magazine company with an offer to subscribe. On the card you're asked to mail back, there's an instruction to peel off a sticker and place it on a particular spot ("Yes, I'll Subscribe" or "No Thanks").

While there may be rare instances where peel-and-stick stickers might actually work for fundraising appeals, I'd steer clear of this technique used by commercial direct mailers. Let me explain why.

In fundraising, you want to acquire as many donors or members as possible. But you're also concerned about acquiring donors who will renew their support year after year. The real value of direct mail — for nonprofit organizations — is that you're acquiring, renewing, *and building relationships* with individuals who will leave your organization a charitable bequest in their wills.

The strategy behind these stickers used in commercial direct mail is that they encourage the recipient to make a decision, to take some action. It's called direct mail because you do want people to respond directly — ideally as soon as they receive your appeal or invitation. And the decision is YES or NO (some have actually tested a third response, "Maybe").

In fundraising, we do want donors to say, "Yes." In fact, our reply devices often begin, "Yes, I want to help ..." But that's just it; the affirmative response is more abstract and less self-interested than with a magazine promotion. In my view, the hard-edge of YES/NO stickers conflicts with the softer, more indirect decision you're asking your donors to make. In a real sense, you hope that if they don't say "Yes" now to your organization, they might do so in the future.

But, perhaps most important, peel-and-stick stickers are just too expensive for most organizations — unless they're mailing at least two- or three-hundred thousand pieces of mail several times a year. Magazines can afford this technique because they're getting the price of the subscription plus the revenue from increased advertising rates (or interest income in the case of credit card promotions).

Yes, in almost all cases, mailings to acquire new donors or members lose money; they're investments in your organization's future. Yet that investment must be kept in balance because those newly acquired donors who go on to make second, third, and more gifts will, in almost all cases, give modest gifts. Fortunately, a precious few will give *lots* more.

So using expensive techniques from commercial direct mail won't help you acquire and renew the overwhelming majority of your members, and those techniques aren't any help with those donors who will be making major gifts.

If you are lucky enough to have funds to risk on fancy techniques, use that money to increase the amount of personalization in mailings to your best donors, and spend the money to attach a live postage stamp to their reply envelope. In fundraising, those two techniques will beat peel-and-stick stickers almost every time.

68.

Do Those Fancy Packages Work?

At my home, I receive some awfully fancy direct mail packages – ones the recipient has to know are produced by sophisticated direct mail firms. Isn't this so-called polished look counterproductive? Don't we run the risk of being perceived by our donors as too slick to be trusted?

For large organizations seeking to involve as many people as possible, these "fancy" packages play an essential role.

Typically, organizations using them mail millions of pieces several times a year. They' re trying to interest and involve those who are "on the margins" of their universe of potential donors or members.

Often these mailings are oversized and the recipient's name is "personalized" in several different places. Typically they have lots of components – two or more letters, decals, postcards, and information slips. In effect, there's something for everyone in these mailings, in the hope that at least some element will catch the reader's attention.

As polished and sophisticated as these mailings look, they are

– in large quantities – relatively inexpensive to mail, compared to more traditional packages. And often these high-visibility mailings generate enough new donors to make the approach worthwhile.

Likewise, there are organizations that have a complicated and arcane mission, one that appeals to a more *limited audience of donors*.

These groups may need to take another approach: using long personalized letters. The outer envelope may also be oversized, with an individually typed label. And inside may be substantial-looking brochures or other inserts that further explain the organization's work. The paper stock may be "classy" and the postage is likely to be first class.

These mailings – often sent to just a few thousand people – are in reality much more expensive on a per unit basis than the over-sized, multi-piece mailings sent out in larger quantity. And even though these mailings don't require complicated printing technology, they involve extensive planning and accomplished writing.

But both approaches do work – in large part precisely because they are polished and sophisticated – but only if your organization's mission and resources make them appropriate.

In direct mail fundraising, one size doesn't fit all. Each organization must craft an approach that's appropriate to its purpose and place. If you're true to what your organization is, donors are smart enough to respond accordingly.

69.

Containing Costs

If your mailing costs are skyrocketing, here are some ways to reduce your costs without jeopardizing the effectiveness of your mailings.

1) Plan a year-long schedule with as many details as possible about the dates for sending out the mailings, the number of pieces to be mailed, the type of envelopes to be used, and any inserts you want to enclose. Use that schedule to negotiate reduced printing costs and to "gang print" any envelopes or other materials that will be used in several mailings (but be careful to avoid ordering too far in advance — envelopes shouldn't sit for more than six months).

2) Spend more money with a professional telephone fundraising firm. This will help you reduce the number of mailings you send out to lapsed or inactive donors, and you'll also get some valuable information about which programs or projects your donors care most about.

3) Reduce the number of mailings sent out to those who consistently make only one gift a year.

4) Use *more* first class postage and reply envelopes with stamps on them for your best donors. Of course, that will increase your postal costs for certain segments of some mailings, but spending money on postage will keep your mailing list much more accurate (saving you money in the long run) and will raise more money for your organization.

5) Don't send out your mailings for bid or print quotes. Instead, find one or two printers and a mailing house that you really like. Treat them like your partners and then work together to reduce costs (and to avoid costly mistakes!).

6) Take advantage of the postal service's deeper discounts for automated (bar-code) pre-sorted mailings. For this to be cost-effective, you'll need to mail a minimum of 4,000 pieces.

7) Give more attention to making address changes quickly to your database. Don't waste money mailing to people whose addresses have changed or who are "undeliverable." (Try to call donors when items are returned "address forwarding expired" — replacing donors who you've lost in this way is very expensive.)

8) Omit inserts from most of your mailings. Brochures, lift letters, and other institutional style inserts often lower response, and they certainly increase your costs.

9) If you're using business reply envelopes (BREs or BRM), test using a "Place Stamp Here" return envelope. That will save you the cost of paying for envelopes that are returned, and, in some cases, your response rate may actually go up.

10) Test short, one-page letters. You may not need to send out four-page letters. For larger mailings to acquire new donors or members, using a very brief letter adds up to considerable savings.

70.

Preferred Postage

For most mailings to most of your donors or prospects, *Nonprofit meter* is the way to go. It usually saves time and money; it often results in first-class treatment by the post office; and recipients frequently fail to notice that it's discounted mail.

When using a meter, you may want to consider having a meter slug added. It's a very small one-time charge to create or purchase a slug. It helps get your organization's message across and it makes your mailing more distinctive.

As always, if you're mailing large enough quantities (5,000 or more of your own donors or 50,000 prospects, you should *test* which works best for you. There are package treatments where for either the sake of appearances or to save costs, a nonprofit stamp, or even a pre-printed indicia, make sense.

VI.

HOW TO ASK

All the guidelines and observations put forth in this book simply set the stage for the main act in direct mail fundraising: asking for the gift.

The primary purpose of your mailing is *not* to impress your readers, nor even to inform them. Your purpose is to get your reader to *respond* – to take a very specific action, namely to mail off a check to your organization.

That will happen consistently only if you explicitly ask for a gift. And it will happen most successfully when you are forth-right in your request. Vague allusions to "financial support" and "your help" will be missed by most of your readers.

It is true that more and more organizations are sending mailings to their donors or members – especially long-time and generous supporters – without any request for a gift. However, these "cultivation mailings" – filled with information and appreciation – take place in the context of mailings that *do* ask for a contribution.

In commercial direct mail, this request for a gift is called the "offer." Apart from the list you mail to, the offer you make has the greatest impact on the rate of return.

In a profit-making scenario, prospects or customers are *offered* certain *benefits* (both tangible and intangible) when they place an order. For those of us in nonprofit organizations, there operates what I call a "philanthropic exchange." Your letter convinces readers that, in exchange for their gifts, they will receive the satisfaction of knowing that certain philanthropic objectives will be achieved (or at least pursued). People in need are helped, children are educated, and values are upheld.

Asking is the part of fundraising that requires the greatest creativity and the most sophistication. To encourage you in this effort, the pages that follow offer suggestions about the amount to request and how to phrase the request.

My hope is that you'll be inspired to create "philanthropic exchanges" that benefit both your organization and the wonderful people who send you the gifts you request.

71.

Ways of Asking for the Gift

"Last year you generously contributed $25 to support our Annual Fund. This year, I hope you'll consider a gift of $50 to help us reach our more ambitious goal."

What you see above is the usual way fund raisers try to encourage donors to give more. It works. Sure. But there are more imaginative ways to ask - *much* more imaginative ways - and my experience shows that they often work better. The ones you see below have brought in direct mail gifts of $100, $1,000, and even $5,000.

Your current donors want to contribute as much as they can to efforts that they feel deserve support. But they need your guidance to know what your organization really needs. If it seems to be $5, they'll send $5 - year after year until you tell them you need $50. Then, with many of them, it will be $50 - year after year.

So, how do you increase giving? Here are six ways to do it:

1) Ask for just one amount - and make it significantly more than the donor's highest previous gift. This may startle the donor, but it will also challenge her to rethink your cause and her giving

patterns.

2) Describe BIG projects - projects with high status and significant impact.

"Our delegation will include members of Congress, business persons and journalists. I hope you will support this dramatic private initiative with a special gift of $1,000."

3) Invite the prospect to be part of a more exclusive group of supporters.

"I am turning to you, and to 25 other special friends of the Center, to ask that you provide leadership gifts of $5,000."

4) Change your language when asking for larger gifts.

"Your gift of $500 will be an investment that will underwrite this project."

5) Offer your donor publicity - recognition for his or her larger contribution. (But be sure to give the donor a chance on the gift card or reply device to make the contribution anonymously. Not everyone likes publicity.)

"When you underwrite this venture with a gift of $1,000, you will be joining others in the film industry as well as leading private citizens. Your name as an Associate Producer will be listed on the credits of this powerful video, as it is distributed across the country!"

6) Take a different tack. Don't ask for a bigger gift. Ask for *more gifts*. For example: increase the number of gifts by using monthly giving options: $20 a month equals $240 a year. Requests for monthly pledges work well in thank-you letters and in appeals to donors who've given you more than one gift.

Only a small percentage of your donors will make monthly pledges. You'll have to wait a few years before there's a meaningful number of monthly donors. But eventually these monthly pledgers will provide a significant portion of your cause's annual income.

"Your generous gift of $20 arrived yesterday, and I'm writing to say how much the Center appreciates it and to assure you that it will have an immediate, positive impact on the children here. But this letter has another purpose, too: To invite you to join the 'Partners in Caring,' a group of donors much like yourself who support the Center with regular monthly gifts. If you could do what you did this month, every month, the impact of your support will be tremendously amplified."

72.

Ask for the Gift Twice or More

After you've written a personal and friendly letter, the only real question left is: "Did you ask for a gift?"

When writing to your upper-level donors, you should send personalized letters that ask for a specific gift amount (or range of gift) ... for a specific purpose ... by a specific date.

Incidentally, the same gift amounts you mention in your letter should appear on the reply device in your mailing package. In other words, the amounts should agree. But be sure, on the reply device, to provide a tick box ([ ] $__) for donors to choose their own gift level.

Unless the letter is just one page, ask for the gift at least twice and probably three times. And do ask for a specific amount. The P.S. is often an ideal place to ask the donor for the gift.

73.

When Not to Ask for a Specific Gift

There are instances when it makes sense to NOT ask for a specific amount — either in your letter or on the reply.

In fact, my sense is that the majority of your letters *shouldn't* ask for a specific amount. Especially when you're sending letters to your current members or donors, you'll find it is more effective to ask for "a generous gift" or a "special gift."

Even when you're writing to prospects or those who've never given, you may wish to be less than specific in your letters, asking the reader to consider *a range* of gift amounts. For example, "Please join the Friends of the Zoo with a membership gift of $25, $50, or $100 if possible." Other groups find it effective in their acquisition letters to ask for an initial gift of "$15 or more."

What these prospect letters try to do by offering a gift range is to set a floor or threshold for initial gifts — and yet allow for those new members or donors who wish to make more significant first gifts to your organization.

Testing for the best initial gift request is perhaps the most important test for any medium- or large-scale direct mail program. Asking too high may dampen response. Asking too low may recruit too many new donors whose subsequent gifts are too small to justify the cost of sending them newsletters and other mailings.

Even though most of your letters won't ask for a particular amount, there are special circumstances when asking for a specific gift can have a tremendous impact on both response rate and the size of gifts you receive:

1) When you're sending personalized letters to your best donors — so that you can refer to the date and amount of their last gift and ask them to match it or give more.

2) When you're sending letters — perhaps pre-printed letters — as part of an annual renewal mailing and want to encourage slightly higher gifts from lower dollar donors (typically those who have never given more than $29 or $34).

3) When you're trying to reactivate lapsed members or donors — especially those who have been generous or have given many gifts. You may ask them to match the specific amount of their last gift or even ask specifically for a lower amount.

4) When a special project or a noteworthy anniversary warrants it, your letter may reference a unique dollar amount — for example, "$55 will provide seeds and tools for a family" or "Please help us celebrate our organization's 80th anniversary by sending a special gift of $80."

Beyond these special situations, most of your fundraising letters will ask the reader to send a contribution, but not suggest a specific amount. That's because, when you're mailing to donors who have made three or fewer gifts in the $10-49 range, it's simply too expensive to personalize letters or to print lots of different versions with specific gift amounts. Very few donors will give larger gifts so the appeal is unlikely to generate enough response and income to pay for the higher costs of using personalization.

Remember, though, that your letter should clearly request a gift, even if the amount is unspecified, and not simply communicate information about your organization or your programs.

And the reply device that accompanies your letter should suggest one, two, or three gift levels. For a person whose highest gift has been $35, you could, for example, have a reply device with $150, $100, and $50. Of course, there should also be a tick box for the donor to write in his or her own amount. Again, only in extraordinary instances, would you give a donor or a member a gift amount lower than his or her previous high gift.

Just as important, your gift requests should be varied throughout the year. Don't send the same donors the same gift requests mailing after mailing. In the course of the year, one or two mailings could ask for ambitious increases in giving levels. At least one mailing a year should make it easy for a member or donor to give exactly what she gave last year. Other mailings, especially renewal mailings, can have reply devices that suggest modest increases in giving.

Because your donors lead busy and complicated lives, *their perceptions about their capacity to give will vary over time.* Direct mail is an effective fund raising tool because it enables you to give a variety of opportunities — at different giving levels and at different times throughout the year — to support your organization.

74.

Pre-Calling Before Sending a Mailing

It's almost always cost-effective to call donors. They're your friends. They care about your organization. Talk with them often.

However, as a fundraising strategy, pre-calling is most effective when you're calling your most generous and responsive donors: those whose last gift is at least $25 and who have given within the last 12 months.

Also, be sure that the solicitation — usually a special appeal mailing — doesn't disappoint the donor. Don't waste pre-calling on a ho-hum project or, God forbid, "the Annual Fund."

Try to call in advance of an appeal letter that describes a major breakthrough ... the launching of a major new program ... or some compelling urgent need that must be addressed.

If you have the right appeal, a pre-calling strategy can become very effective if you also call the donors again — after the letter has gone out. At that point, your call is to make sure they received the letter and to seek a specific financial commitment.

Of course, this phone-mail-phone strategy is expensive. So, once again, be sure you're focusing on your most responsive and generous donors. Perhaps, in this instance, you'll want to reach only your $100-plus donors.

Pre-calling is successful in special circumstances. But, in general and especially with less responsive donors, our experience has been that calling after a letter has been sent is just as effective — or even more effective — than calling before a mailing.

75.

Credit Card Option

At our firm, we have conducted several different tests involving credit card options. In almost every case, the option *fails* to increase response rates or boost average gifts. In some instances, the credit card test panel has performed *worse*.

But I do know of some organizations and some instances where the credit card option has worked. My somewhat eclectic review of direct mail appeals leads me to believe that annual membership appeals use this option. The demographics of the membership (younger, more affluent, highly educated) may make credit card use more acceptable.

Remember, though, in general, *fundraising is old-fashioned*. It is *not* the same as commercial direct mail merchandising. Your challenge is to communicate credibility and trustworthiness.

Donors want to know that their charitable gifts will be used to achieve the greatest impact. And many donors derive great satisfaction in taking out their checkbook, writing out your organization's name and the dollar amount of their gift, tearing the check out of the checkbook, and inserting it along with the reply device in the envelope you provide.

My sense is that offering to take credit cards undercuts this philanthropic process.

However, in sustainer or pledge programs, credit cards can be a great way for donors who want to make monthly gifts. And it's absolutely wonderful if you offer the option of making credit card gifts for phone-in contributions in memorial/tribute programs.

76.

Increasing the Key First Gift

The average gift you receive in response to prospect or acquisition mailings is a predictor of the level of future gifts. In fact, testing the requested gift amounts is the most important of all tests for prospect mailings.

That's because, in general, when you *lower* the minimum gift you request (for example, from $25 to $12), your response rate goes *up*. And sometimes you get very lucky and the average gift doesn't decline — even though you're asking for less.

But even if the average gift does go down, the increased response rate is great enough to generate total income greater than if you had a higher average gift but a lower response rate. The net effect is that your prospect mailings look strong and your donor database grows more quickly.

Of course, one of the terrible truths of fundraising is that very few donors ever increase the dollar amount of their contributions over and above their initial gifts. A donor whose first gift is $15 will most likely never write you a check for more than $15.

The good news is that a precious few do make dramatic increases in their giving level, another goodly number make several gifts a year, and a meaningful number go on to leave sizable charitable bequests.

Adding to the fundraising challenge is that — again, in general — the higher the initial gift the greater the probability that a new donor or member will make subsequent gifts. Thus, if you have lots of donors or members who join with an initial gift of $10, your renewal or retention rates will be lower than if those initial gifts were $20 or $25.

Still more challenging is that even with strong response rates from new $10 and $15 donors in response to *renewal* mailings or special appeals, the income contributed usually doesn't offset the cost of mailing to that segment of donors. For renewal or re-solicitation mailings to generate net income, you'll need to get at least a six percent response rate if you're a medium sized organization (10,000 to 100,000 donors) and you're mailing to donors with average gifts of $10 or 15.

So after you've weighed all the advantages and disadvantages of lowering gift requests to generate response rates, you may wish to boost gift amounts in acquisition. Here are some techniques that are worth testing:

1) Select prospect lists from organizations that have higher gift levels, and use subscription and homeowner lists which tend to generate higher average gifts.

2) Circle a second and higher dollar amount on the reply device, and add a brief handwritten note such as, "A gift in this amount will really help!"

3) Pick an odd amount — $28 or $33, for example — and let the prospective donor know what this gift amount will accom-

plish: "Your gift of $33 will provide seeds and planting supplies for school children."

4) In some cases, a longer (and more factual, informative) letter will result in a higher average gift.

5) First class postage and personalization can increase average gift amounts, but be careful since these both really bump up mailing costs.

6) Offering a premium for gifts made at a certain level will sometimes increase an average gift. But premiums can also reduce response rates and lower average gifts (some prospective donors actually don't like premiums!).

77.

Big Gifts by Mail

Every once in a while someone at our firm begins to worry that others will start copying our highly effective high-dollar mailings. I'm not concerned at all. In fact, I'll share several of our secrets with you — confident you *won't* have the nerve to try them. That's because you'll need to spend $5 to $10, and maybe even $15, on a package to secure a $1,000 gift.

I don't know many executive directors or development committees willing to stomach $5 or more per package. Also, when you send these expensive mailings, you'll get lots of complaints from donors — and you know how staff and board members love those!

But, just in case you're blessed with an understanding boss or board, here are some of the elements of effective high-dollar mailings:

1) Use first-class postage on the outer envelope and a live-stamped return envelope. If your piece weighs two to three ounces, that's more than a dollar just for postage.

2) Personalize (usually with a laser printer) the outer envelope, the first (and perhaps second) page of the letter, and — don't

skip this one — the reply device. That's another 25 to 50 cents.

3) Use high-quality laid stock for the letter (and it will need to be a three-, four-, five-, or even six-page letter if you want to get big gifts) and the reply device. Printing costs for the letter, outer envelope (often over-sized), brochure or other insert, reply device, and reply envelope can easily add another $1.00 to $3.00 per package.

4) Unlike high-volume membership acquisition mailings, inserts are sometimes very helpful in high-dollar appeals. A special brochure, a newsclip or a fact sheet can support the main argument of the letter. Another 10 to 50 cents.

5) These mailings have to be hand-assembled — to make sure all the personalized pieces go to the *same* individual. This is too important a task for volunteers, so you'll need to budget 30 to 50 cents per package for hand-matched lettershop services.

Of course, the most important factor in determining whether you secure $1,000 gifts is sending these expensive packages to the right donors. In general, select donors who have *previously* made single gifts of $100 or more to your organization.

With *very* careful list selection (no, not wealthy homeowners — and, please, no lists of attorneys or doctors) you can sometimes send these high-dollar packages to individuals who have never given before.

78.

Attracting Larger First Gifts

Here's a direct mail fundraising truth: the higher the initial gift the greater the probability a new donor or member will make subsequent gifts.

Let me explain why and suggest steps you can take to attract the largest possible first gift.

Typically, 30 to 40 percent of those who make an initial gift will go on to make additional gifts (usually at the same level). That's good news, of course. Even better news is that, *on average*, almost all donors increase their level of giving.

If that sounds a bit confusing, here's an example. If you acquire 1,000 new donors whose initial gift is just $10, about 30 to 40 percent of them will make a subsequent gift. And, as a *group*, their *average* gift will increase to $13.00. In other words, a sufficient number of these donors will make second gifts of $15, $25, or more, so that the *average* second gift is now higher, if only by a little.

But that's the problem, isn't it? For most organizations, that kind of response and average gift doesn't pay for the cost of mailing and maintaining those donors whose first gift is $10.

Fortunately, the same dynamic operates for higher level givers. Those who make initial gifts of $100 will make subsequent gifts and will also increase their support. It's easy to see that $130 average gift beats that $13 gift hands down. (And, yes, the higher the initial gift, the more likely it is the donor will give a second gift because these donors receive more mailings and more personalized ones.)

Nevertheless, the reality is that four to five times more individuals will send $10, $15 or $25 than will make a first gift of $100. So it's impossible to acquire donors *only* at the higher level (the very nature of philanthropy, which *is* voluntary giving, is that individuals who care about your organization will give in the amount *they* feel is appropriate).

Thus, it's a mistake to try to acquire new donors only at the highest possible level only. Rather, through careful testing, you should see what initial gift amount attracts the largest number of new donors – $15, $20, $25, or perhaps $35. Then, when the exceptional individual sends in that first gift of $100 or more, take extraordinary efforts to thank and cultivate that new donor or member.

If you find you're acquiring lots of $10 and $15 new donors, you can take three actions: a) send a thank you that allows the new donor to make a subsequent gift right away; b) invite those new donors to become monthly donors – 12 gifts of $10 adds up to $120; and c) include those donors in subsequent acquisition mailings, which are low cost and which may inspire the individual to "rejoin" at a higher gift level.

79.

Seeking Stretch Gifts

One of the most terrible truths about direct mail fundraising is that very, very few donors ever increase the size of the original gift they sent. In fact, most send gift amounts that are *lower* than their highest gift.

However, the wonderful news – the secret power source of nonprofit fund raising – is that a handful of extraordinary individuals *will* increase their gift levels, and do so dramatically. Just think about the impact of the one of 100 donors who goes from $100 to $1000. That increase raises the average gift of all the others who don't give more.

The other very good news is that a meaningful percentage – somewhere between 10 and 20 percent of direct mail donors – will give *more than one gift a year*. So the member who refuses to increase her gift from $35 to $50 is, fortunately, willing to make two additional gifts throughout the year of $25. Thus her annual giving is $85 – a lot more than $50.

And perhaps the best news yet is that about five percent of your donors can be persuaded to send a contribution *every month*. Most of them will pre-authorize their banks or credit cards to send their gift to you directly. You may be frustrated that your "$25 donor" won't "upgrade" by sending a $100 check. But if that faithful friend sends you 12 gifts of just $20, that's a whopping $240.

The conclusions I hope you'll draw are:

1) Some of your mailings should ask for stretch gifts, and,

2) The best way to stretch a donor's giving – especially when they're giving less than $50 – is to recruit them as monthly donors. In a real sense, you're asking these donors to make an even *smaller* contribution – but to make it every month.

By planning your annual mailing schedule carefully and by using personalization wisely, you'll discover there really are no small gifts when it comes to raising money through the mail.

80.

Asking for Monthly Gifts and Charitable Bequests

As I've emphasized several times in this book, a terrible truth of direct mail fundraising is that the overwhelming majority of donors won't make gifts much greater than their initial gift. Once a $25 donor, always a $25 donor — or at best, $35 or $50 every once in a while.

That's true even when you know donors are wealthy. There's something about a donor's perception of what his or her appropriate gift is, and it's very difficult to budge him or her from this amount — no matter how much money the individual has.

Still, the good news is that a fabulous few do make the leap, so be sure to plan on sending out in the course of a year one, two, or three "high-dollar appeals."

Since donors don't normally upgrade to larger gifts, you have to persuade them to give *more than one gift a year*. One of the best ways to do this is to recruit the three to five percent of your members who are willing to make *monthly* gifts to your organization.

Often called sustainers, these monthly donors (or pledgers, as they're sometimes called) can produce enormous revenue at very low cost — once you make the big initial investment to recruit them (it will take several mailings and telephone calls if not a professional firm).

Credit card and electronic funds transfer are two methods offered by many organizations that seek monthly gifts. A "paper" reminder system is usually necessary for those donors who don't want to give out credit card numbers or are uncomfortable having their bank accounts debited each month.

But the most effective way, in the long term, to raise more money from your members is to begin promoting *charitable bequests* — in your newsletter, your thank-you program, and with special mailings three or four times a year to selected, long-time members.

I see instances again and again of donors or members who have faithfully given $15, $25, or $50 each year — and then in their wills leave bequests of five and six figures. In fact, for both the donor (who may have saved his or her heirs estate taxes) and for your organization, charitable bequests are truly a big benefit of an ongoing membership program.

81.

Increasing Credibility and Accountability

In the nonprofit community today, we hear a lot about the need to be accountable and transparent. With respect to direct mail, the best antidote to donor skepticism is to send out friendly, informative – and quick — thank you letters. In most cases, those who send gifts have transcended society's cynicism. These exceptional individuals deserve your sincere gratitude.

A thank you letter is also an excellent vehicle for being accountable for the use of contributed funds. In it, you can refer to a specific program or project – or better yet, recent accomplishment or noteworthy result – made possible by the donor's financial support.

Some organizations include inserts along with their thank yous. If appropriate, one of these could be a simple summary of your organization's annual income and expenses. This insert, which shouldn't be elaborate or expensive, can also offer a copy of your most recently audited financial statement. You might title the piece,

"We use your contributions wisely" or "How we put your gifts to work."

Such an insert is especially important when thanking first-time donors. Elsewhere in this book, we've talked about *welcome packages* – a packet or set of materials sent to new donors in addition to their initial thank you letter.

New donors are taking a chance that yours is an effective organization, and – short of sending them a week's worth of reading material – you should let these new supporters know they've made a good investment.

In addition to including brief financial information, your welcome packet might have a listing of staff members who can be contacted for more information. You might also want to list your top accomplishments of last year, as well as any endorsements or testimonials. Your welcome package should also give the new donor an opportunity to request a copy of your most recent annual report.

Annual reports are strong conveyors of accountability because they do include your financial statements – or summarized financial information. In addition, you have a chance to review your organization's accomplishments, identify your board of directors, and acknowledge your major donors and other funders. Just seeing the names of those who support you should be very reassuring to all your donors.

Finally, your appeal letters can themselves reflect a sense of accountability and transparency. I don't recommend you use financial information or boast about your low fundraising costs in your appeals. These are supposed be friendly and enthusiastic letters – not accounting documents.

But your letters should talk about your organization's effectiveness, about the results that you are achieving. And one of the most compelling cases you can make for sending a gift is when you can tell a donor what a specific contribution will make possible.

Letters that talk about results and about what gifts will accomplish are even more powerful fund raising tools when you remember to be effusive in your thanks for the donor's past support.

Also by Emerson & Church

FUND RAISING REALITIES EVERY BOARD MEMBER MUST FACE

A 1-Hour Crash Course on Raising Major Gifts
by David Lansdowne, 112 pp. $24.95

If every board member of every nonprofit organization across America read this book, it's no exaggeration to say that millions upon millions of additional dollars would be raised.

How could it be otherwise when, after spending just *one* hour with this gem, board members everywhere would understand virtually everything they need to know about raising major gifts. Not more, not less. Just exactly what they need to do to be successful.

In his book, *Fund Raising Realities Every Board Member Must Face: A 1-Hour Crash Course on Raising Major Gifts for Nonprofit Organizations*, David Lansdowne has distilled the essence of major gifts fund raising, put it in the context of 47 "realities," and delivered it in unfailingly clear prose.

Nothing about this book will intimidate board members. It is brief, concise, easy to read and free of all jargon. Further, it is a work that motivates, showing as it does just how doable raising big money is.

The appeal of *Fund Raising Realities* is that Lansdowne addresses every important principle and technique of fund raising, and explains them in a succinct way board members will grasp immediately.

In other words, *Fund Raising Realities* puts everyone on a level playing field - board member with board member, and board member with staff.

Companion Book to Fund Raising Realities

ASKING

A 59-Minute Guide to Everything Board Members, Volunteers, & Staff Must Know to Secure the Gift
by Jerold Panas, 112 pp. $24.95

It ranks right up there with public speaking. Nearly all of us fear it. And yet it is critical to our success.

Asking for money. It makes even the stout-hearted quiver.

But now comes a new book, *Asking: A 59-Minute Guide to Everything Board Members, Staff and Volunteers Must Know to Secure the Gift*. And short of a medical elixir, it's the next best thing for emboldening you, your board members and volunteers to ask with skill, finesse ... and powerful results.

Jerold Panas, who as a staff person, board member and volunteer has secured gifts ranging from $50 to $50 million, understands the art of asking perhaps better than anyone in America.

He knows what makes donors tick, he's intimately familiar with the anxieties of board members, and he fully understands the frustrations and exigencies of staff.

He has harnessed all of this knowledge and experience and produced what many are already calling a landmark book.

What *Asking* convincingly shows — and one reason staff will applaud the book and board members will devour it — is that it doesn't take stellar communication skills to be an effective asker.

Nearly everyone, regardless of their persuasive ability, can become an effective fundraiser if they follow a few step-by-step guidelines.

You have to know your cause, of course, and be committed to it. But, nearly as important, you have to know how to get the appointment, how to present your case, how to read your donor's words, how to handle objections, how to phrase your request, and even what behaviors to avoid.

Panas mines all of this territory, and because he speaks directly from his heart to the heart of board members, staff, and volunteers, the advice is authentic, credible, and ultimately inspiring.

For Developing Your Board

THE ULTIMATE BOARD MEMBER'S BOOK

A 1-Hour Guide to Understanding and Fulfilling Your Role and Responsibilities
by Kay Sprinkel Grace, 120 pp., $24.95

Here is a book for *all* nonprofit boards:

• Those wanting to operate with maximum effectiveness,

• Those needing to clarify exactly what their job is, and,

• Those wanting to ensure that all members — novice and veteran — are 'on the same page' with respect to their role and responsibilities

Kay Sprinkel Grace's new work will take your board members only one hour to read, and yet they'll come away from *The Ultimate Board Member's Book* with a solid command of just what they need to do to help your organization succeed.

It's all here in jargon-free language: how boards work, what the job entails, the time commitment, the role of staff, serving on committees and task forces, fundraising responsibilities, conflicts of interest, group decision-making, effective recruiting, de-enlisting board members, board self-evaluation, and more.

In sum, everything a board member needs to know to understand their role and serve capably is explored.

Showing admirable restraint, Grace resists overloading the reader, as Michael Byram, President of the University of Colorado Foundation, attests: "*Ultimate* provides the most *succinct*, yet *thorough*, explanation of the responsibilities of a nonprofit board member I've yet read."

Real world, not theoretical, concrete not abstract, *The Ultimate Board Member's Book* focuses on issues and concerns that all board members will inevitably face and grapple with.

A 'How-to' Classic

THE RELENTLESSLY PRACTICAL GUIDE TO RAISING SERIOUS MONEY
Proven Techniques for Nonprofit Organizations
by David Lansdowne, 2nd Edition, 240 pp. , $24.95

Why of all the hundreds of fund raising books available did Americorps Vista, with offices throughout the U.S., single out *The Relentlessly Practical Guide to Fundraising* as the premier book on the subject and provide a copy to thousands of its staff?

Read David Lansdowne's acclaimed work and you'll quickly understand why. No other writer in the field is as succinct, yet comprehensive. Nor do others have Lansdowne's trademark gift of extracting the essence of a technique and illuminating it in unfailingly clear prose.

Lansdowne plumbs *every* major aspect of fundraising: from annual campaigns to capital campaigns, from major gifts to Internet fundraising, from planned giving to direct mail to prospect research.

Each chapter is delivered with heat-seeking precision. For example, do you want to know how to establish a gift club for donors? Turn to that chapter and chances are you'll learn more in the nine pages than you would from reading an entire book on the subject.

The same goes for attracting corporate support. Yes, you could spend hours boning up on the topic. But there's no need, as Lansdowne discusses everything you should know in a mere 11 pages.

There are other standout chapters that lift this book above others.

"The 16 Best Pieces of Fundraising Advice" may be the best rendering of its kind put to pen.

"Fundraising's 20 Biggest Mistakes" is a masterful discussion that alerts you to each and every red flag.

"Fundraising Myths" explores more than a dozen pernicious myths that many still labor under.

And, "What Every Board Member Must Know to Succeed," should be required reading for any trustee serving a gift-supported organization.

Here's pragmatic guidance you can put into practice literally today.